COTSWOLD LANDSCAPES

COTSWOLD

LANDSCAPES

PHOTOGRAPHS BY ROB TALBOT

TEXT BY ROBIN WHITEMAN

First published in Great Britain in 1999
by Weidenfeld & Nicolson

Paperback edition first published in 2000 by
Seven Dials.

Published in 2004 by Silverdale Books
An imprint of Bookmart Limited
Registered Number 2372865
Trading as Bookmart Limited
Blaby Road
Wigston
Leicestershire LE18 4SE

A CIP catalogue record for this book is
available from the British Library
ISBN 1 84509 010 1

Designed by: Harry Green
Map Created by: Technical Art Services
Edited by: Jonathan Hilton
Printed and Bound in Italy
Set in Baskerville and MetaPlus

PHOTOGRAPHS
page 1: Cottages, Hidcote Bartrim
page 2: Cleeve Cloud, Cleeve Hill
page 6: Broadway Tower

NOTE

Since there is general disagreement about the
precise limits of the Cotswolds, for the purpose
of this book the limestone has been allowed to
dictate the boundaries. Oxford may not be
technically part of the region, but many of its
churches, colleges and houses are built of
Cotswold stone, and, therefore, the city seems
an appropriate point from which to start. The
most northerly point of the Cotswolds is Meon
Hill, a few miles north of Chipping Campden.
Bath and Bradford-on-Avon mark the
southernmost extremities. The westernmost
boundary is clearly marked by the steep
limestone escarpment, sweeping, as it does,
from Broadway Hill south-westward for some
forty miles (above Cheltenham, Gloucester
and Stroud) to Dursley, and then southward
for a further twenty miles to Bath. The eastern
boundary is less precise, but includes, from
south to north, Castle Combe, Malmesbury,
Fairford, Kelmcott, Woodstock, Great Tew,
Long Compton, Moreton-in-Marsh and
Ilmington. Those English counties included
within these limits are a large part of
Gloucestershire (east and south), Bath and
North East Somerset, a sliver of north-west
Wiltshire, north Oxfordshire (north of the
upper Thames valley and south-west of
Banbury), a small corner of southern
Warwickshire, and an even tinier portion
of Worcestershire (namely Broadway and
Broadway Hill).

So as not to undermine the noble status
of a 1,000-foot mountain by making it a lowly
304.79-metre hill, all measurements are
imperial. Feet can be converted to metres,
however, by dividing by 3.281.

ACKNOWLEDGEMENTS

Robin Whiteman and Rob Talbot would
particularly like to acknowledge the generous
co-operation they received from English
Heritage (South East & South West Regions)
and the National Trust (Severn, Wessex and
Thames & Chilterns Regional Offices).
Particular thanks go to Robert Morris,
Manager of the National Trust Photographic
Library. We are also extremely grateful to
the following: His Grace the Duke of
Marlborough (Blenheim Palace); The Curator
of the Roman Baths Museum & Pump Room;
the Curators of the Sheldonian Theatre,
Oxford; photographs of Sudeley Castle and
Gardens reproduced by kind permission of
Sudeley Castle; Kelmscott Manor was
photographed with the permission of The
Society of Antiquaries of London; Forestry
Commission, Westonbirt Arboretum;
Mr & Mrs Gorton, Managers of Broadway
Tower Country Park. Our appreciation also
extends to all those individuals and
organizations too numerous to mention
by name who, nevertheless, have made such
a valuable contribution to this book.

CONTENTS

STANDING ON THE SUMMIT OF Beacon Hill, more than 1,000 feet above sea-level, Broadway Tower seems to epitomize much that is characteristically Cotswold. Despite its untraditional design, the structure is built of oolitic limestone, and, therefore, possesses that timeless quality so typical of the architecture of the region. Its colourful history embraces tragedy, romance, mystery and tradition, while famous people associated with the stone tower include James Wyatt, the neo-Gothic architect, William Morris, the artist, writer, craftsman and socialist, Edward Burne-Jones, the Victorian painter and designer, and Dante Gabriel Rossetti, the Pre-Raphaelite artist and poet. The hilltop itself, as well as overlooking the famous village of Broadway, offers magnificent views over a dozen or more counties, as well as embracing scenery of remarkable richness and variety.

The sixty-five-feet-high tower, billed as 'the highest little castle in the Cotswolds', stands within the Broadway Tower Country Park – containing a rare breed of sheep known as Cotswold Lions, a herd of red deer and a motley assortment of domesticated animals, including highland cattle and llamas. Yet, despite the wide range of attractions, it is the Park's spectacular hilltop location (in a designated Area of Outstanding Natural Beauty: the Cotswolds) that makes so memorable and rewarding an impression – even in the most extreme weather conditions.

During the production of this book and our 'Country Series' volume *The Cotswolds* (first published in 1987), Rob and I have experienced Cotswold weather in all its seasons and moods: from the freak and sudden blizzard of winter 1986, when Beacon or Broadway Hill turned white and a sub-zero wind froze the molecules in one of Rob's photographic filters, rendering it useless, to the heavy cloudburst of summer 1998, which (by somehow managing to avoid obscuring the sun) produced myriad tiny rainbows that danced and played on the bumpers, bonnets and roofs of vehicles travelling along the Fosse Way – the old Roman road that runs the entire length of the region. Even on bright, sunny, cloudless days, the wind can blow so fierce that, as C Henry Warren noted in *A Cotswold Year* (1936):

'you only had to wet your finger to taste the salt that had been blown in from the sea a good thirty miles away.'

Among the fascinating snippets of information on display inside Broadway Tower is an account of a milkmaid, wearing voluminous skirts, who was lifted bodily into the air by a great gust of wind and carried some distance across Broadway Hill, before being deposited back on the ground in a thornbush. During one such blustery day, Rob was trying to take photographs on Peaked Down, near Dursley, when a powerful gust ripped his tripod out of the ground – in which it had been firmly secured (or so he thought) – and carried it and the camera some twelve feet before dumping the whole caboodle back on the ground in an ungainly and crumpled heap. More often than not, however, Cotswold weather is damp, overcast and heavy, with lingering mist or poor visibility. In *Rural Rides*, William Cobbett wrote of the region in 1826:

'The high lands always, during the year, and especially during the summer, receive much more of rain than the low lands. The clouds hang about the hills, and the dews, when they rise, go, most frequently, and cap the hills.'

Yet, when the sun does shine, the glory and mystery of the limestone is sensationally revealed. For, as J B Priestley observed in *English Journey* (1934), walls and buildings made from this luminous stone:

'knew the trick of keeping the lost sunlight of centuries glimmering about them.'

Although the stone of Broadway Tower came from quarries further east, and is, therefore, somewhat darker than local material, most of the oolitic limestone used in the region's buildings is dug out of the ground on site, or close by. This use of local, rather than imported, building material has made Cotswold architecture – whether it is barn, cottage, manor, church or drystone wall – blend into the landscape and appear a natural and an organic part of it, rather than stand out as something distinctly alien and intrusive.

The rock, composed of lime from the powdered shells of primitive sea organisms, is part of a belt of Jurassic limestone that stretches north-east from the coast of Dorset to the coast of Yorkshire. In the Cotswolds, the rock – varying subtly in colour and texture from one area to the next and of irregular thickness – forms a steep escarpment, or 'edge', in the west. This edge, reaching its highest in the north between Cleeve Hill and Broadway Hill, is capped with Inferior (lower or older) Oolite, below which are even older layers of sandstones and clays. Despite the fact that the younger bed of Great Oolite, which was formed above the Inferior Oolite, has been completely removed by erosion on the western scarp, the tilting and dipping of the strata towards the east has meant that large areas of Great Oolite still exist in the central Cotswolds.

Although workable stone can be found in certain strata within the Inferior Oolite series, it is the Great Oolite series that yields the finest building material. Lying close to the surface in places such as Bourton-on-the-Water and, therefore, readily available, the limestone is comparatively soft when first quarried and, as such, is easily carved or sawn. On being exposed to the air, it gradually hardens and loses its pale, creamy-buff colour, mellowing into a range of colours that are almost impossible to describe: ever-changing, shifting subtly from one moment to the next with each variation in weather and light. Nevertheless, as a general rule: in the north of the region, around Broadway, the colour of the stone appears a deep gold; to the east, towards Oxford, it is a darker orange; to the west, around Painswick, it is a silver-grey; and in the south, near Bath, it takes on a honey-cream colour. Some of the limestone is rich in fossils, especially around Stonesfield (noted for its high-quality roofing stone), where the village, as Arthur Mee pointed out in *Oxfordshire* (1942):

> 'is an immense cemetery of giant reptiles, sea lizards, turtles, creatures of the marshes, and teeth of sharks which swam primeval seas.'

Indeed, it was through the presence of fossils in rock strata that William Smith, the 'Father of British Geology', was able to produce his classic geological map of England, Wales and part of Scotland in 1815. His work as an engineer, carrying out surveys for the construction of canals and bridges, took him the length and breadth of the country. Keeping detailed drawings and records of his observations, he was the first to recognize that different types of rock strata could be dated by the sets of fossils they

contained. A large stone monolith, which was erected in 1891, commemorates 'Strata' Smith's pioneering work in the field of British geology. It stands in the Oxfordshire-Cotswold village of Churchill, where he was born in 1769.

The use of Cotswold limestone not only affects the shape of the landscape and the nature of the soil, it also brings – unlike other areas outside the region where alien building material has been

Occupying the sides of a deep valley, west of Fossebridge, Chedworth is an ancient village with a church dating from Norman times. Dedicated to St Andrew, the building is noted for its striking Perpendicular façade (including windows), constructed in the fifteenth century when the prosperity of the Cotswold wool trade was at its height. At the head of the wooded valley to the north-west are the remains of a Romano-British villa, Chedworth Roman Villa (now owned by the National Trust). The site was discovered by accident in 1864, when a gamekeeper found fragments of mosaic and pottery in the vicinity of a rabbit warren. Subsequent excavations unearthed the foundations of a building complex dating from between the early second century AD to the late fourth century AD. The mock-Tudor house and museum nearby dates from the Victorian period.

introduced – beauty and harmony to every field, town and village. Every building, whether a humble cottage, a grand mansion or a magnificent church, is constructed from the same oolitic stone, giving them a visual affinity with each other and the landscape that is found nowhere else in England. Indeed, the buildings of the region have an architectural style – a form of simplified Gothic – that is unique. Known as Cotswold vernacular, it has dominated almost every building – from the smallest to the largest – for centuries. It has survived, with only slight modifications, the Italian influence of the Renaissance period and the changing fashions of both Georgian and Victorian times.

The style was perfected after the Dissolution (notably in Elizabethan and Jacobean times), when the masons that had previously worked for the monasteries were forced to find alternative employment in towns and villages. Constructing a whole range of buildings, including farmhouses and barns, they produced a basic design that was dictated by the properties of the stone: solid foundations, sturdy walls and steep-pitched roofs. The main design features were dormers, gables, heavy square chimney stacks and small windows with mullions, transoms and drip mouldings. Variations within this basic formula, however – in size and stature, as well as in embellishment – allowed each building to assert its own unique individuality and character, while retaining its part in a harmonious whole. This brought about a unity with neighbouring structures and, especially, with the surrounding landscape from which the stone originally came. As Alec Clifton-Taylor wrote in *The Pattern of English Building* (1987):

'Nothing is more striking about Cotswold buildings than the visual accord which they achieve with the landscape in which they are placed . . . In the Cotswolds the buildings themselves, even the barns, are of such high quality that at every turn it is they that we notice first. The landscape here plays second fiddle: it is the background, the *mise-en-scène*, the frame. That is why, for those who cherish our building heritage, the Cotswolds occupy a special place.'

The roofs of traditional Cotswold buildings are steeply pitched for two reasons: to support the heavy weight of the 'slates', and to encourage the rain to flow quickly away, thereby preventing the water from penetrating the porous limestone. As the steep pitch of the roof does not leave space for windows under the eaves, the problem of admitting natural light to the uppermost rooms was solved by topping the walls with miniature gables, in which a window was inserted to form a dormer. The drip mouldings, or stone projections, found over the windows and doors are designed to stop the rainwater from penetrating the walls below. Some of the drip courses, especially on ecclesiastical buildings, were decorated with carved heads or other types of embellishment. Yet, as Edith Brill observed in *Life and Tradition on the Cotswolds* (1973), despite the changing whims of fashion:

'Only the incidentals, the windows, porches and ornament, were changed to suit the period, and as it is the nature of oolitic limestone to take all styles to itself the unity remained for the most part unspoilt.'

As a rule, however, Cotswold builders favoured simplicity rather than adornment. Indeed, as Brill remarked, it is the earliest buildings, those constructed before the end of the eighteenth century:

'before the style became pompous, which achieve the greatest elegance and charm, kept in bounds by a certain austerity of line and ornament. Today time has weathered them into an intrinsic adornment of the whole building. There is a certain reticence in a Cotswold building as there is in a Cotswold landscape and the old craftsmen were instinctively aware of this and never overloaded their work with ornament.'

The use of oolitic limestone as a building material was not restricted to the Cotswolds, however. Quarries, especially those having access to the canal and waterway transport system of the River Thames and its tributaries, shipped stone not only east to Oxford and London, but also west to Gloucester and Bristol. In *The Hidden Landscape* (1993), Richard Fortey noted a large Cotswold-stone house by the Thames at Maidenhead, commenting that:

'a building of rough stone which might have slipped away unnoticed near Malmesbury, is here miles and miles from its geological home, and serves only as an object lesson in how buildings should spring from the geology beneath them.'

Unlike today, the master masons of the past were often as highly regarded and well known as the architects. Indeed, many were better qualified, given that their craft had been learned over a long and rigorous apprenticeship. As well, they invariably possessed some form of 'secret' or 'sacred' knowledge of geometry, knowledge that was kept exclusively within the family and passed from father to son, down through the generations. Among the most celebrated of the master masons in the Cotswolds were Thomas Strong (1632–81) and Christopher ('Kit') Kempster (1626–1715), both of whom owned quarries above the Windrush valley, near Burford. They also worked closely with one of England's greatest architects, Sir Christopher Wren.

Strong was the grandson of Timothy Strong, who moved north from Wiltshire during the reign of James I to establish quarries at Little Barrington and Taynton, thereby founding the family firm. Little is known about Kempster's early years, except that he came from a family of Cotswold yeoman farmers. His quarries, now long abandoned and overgrown, were located behind the family farmhouse at Upton, just north-west of Burford. Both men supplied stone for the rebuilding of London after the Great Fire of 1666, and both contributed material to the rebuilding of St Paul's Cathedral.

Architecturally, compared with Wren's domed masterpiece, Broadway Tower pales almost into insignificance. Yet its designer, James Wyatt (1746–1813), was one of the most fashionable and highly influential English architects of his day. Although he worked in the neo-classical style, Wyatt is chiefly remembered for his neo-Gothic country houses, notably the spectacular Fonthill Abbey in Wiltshire (demolished after the collapse of its great central tower, and subsequent ruin). However, his ruthless 'restorations' and 'improvements' to cathedrals, such as Durham, Salisbury, Hereford and Lichfield, earned him the name of 'Wyatt the Destroyer'.

It was while he was working at Croome Court, near Worcester, for George William, 6th Earl of Coventry, that Wyatt produced his plan and elevation for a 'Saxon Tower' on Beacon Hill. Now known as 'Broadway Tower', the basic structure was six-sided with a round turret at each of three alternate corners. Embellishments on the final building included battlements, balconies, gargoyles and a mixture of windows – large, round and small (but none divided vertically by stone mullions as shown

in the original plan). Apparently, the decision to use a stone darker than that found locally was 'to enhance the illusion that the new building was a sombre antique'.

Although the tower is generally considered to be a Romantic folly, erected at a time when picturesque ruins and mock-castles were fashionable on country estates, several alternative reasons have been put forward to explain why it was built on its prominent hilltop site. The most practical is connected with Broadway Hill being one of an ancient chain of beacon sites – stretching the entire length and breadth of the island – on which fires were lit for speedy communication, especially in times of danger (such as the approach of the Spanish Armada in 1588). The Earl of Coventry, in fact, had two Worcestershire estates, Croome Court and Spring Hill (Broadway Hill being part of the latter). Putting both facts together, it has been suggested that the tower was constructed primarily as a signal station, so that the staff at Spring Hill could warn Croome Court that the Earl, or members of his family, had left and preparations should be set in motion for their imminent arrival.

Another possible reason is that the tower was built as a hunting lodge and vantage point from which the Earl's second wife, and her entourage, could watch the hunt when it met on the Spring Hill estate.

Over time, apparently, the local villagers and farmers forgot that the tower had been erected at the close of the eighteenth century by the Earl of Coventry, and they began to attribute its presence in the landscape to more ancient builders. One story, according to information inside the tower, claimed that it had been built:

'in some distant pagan past for a man with three wives – one for each turret.'

Whatever the theories and stories regarding its original purpose, there is no doubt that the views from the top of the tower – 1,089 feet above sea-level – are particularly extensive. Indeed, it is claimed that a quarter of the total number of counties in England and Wales can be seen on a clear day. Among the numerous towns, cities and villages that can be discerned with the naked eye, or with the aid of a telescope, are: Evesham and Pershore, watered by the Warwickshire Avon; Coventry, with its three renowned spires; Birmingham, spread out across the

All Souls College,
Oxford

northern horizon (invariably, under a band of haze); Stratford-upon-Avon, renowned worldwide as the birthplace of William Shakespeare; Warwick, with its magnificent medieval castle; Royal Leamington Spa, boasting elegant Regency and early Victorian architecture; Stow-on-the-Wold, 'where the wind blows cold'; and, immediately below the tower, that 'showpiece' of the Cotswolds, Broadway, its houses and cottages dropping abruptly down into the vale from the lower slopes of the Cotswold escarpment. The ancient market town of Chipping Campden, dominated by its magnificent 'wool' church, also lies within sight, nestling in a hollow between the hills, three miles to the north-east.

The steep and irregular weather-beaten edge, which overlooks the broad, flat valleys of the Avon and Severn and clearly delineates the western limit of the Cotswold plateau all the way south to Bath, can be discerned over a distance of some twenty miles, from Meon Hill – its northernmost extremity – to Cleeve Hill, above Cheltenham. This is its highest point, reaching 1,084 feet above sea-level.

Most prominent among the oolitic limestone outliers, which rise from the level plain like tiny islands in a sea of patchwork green, is Bredon Hill, topped by the earthwork remains of an Iron Age fort and an eighteenth-century stone edifice, known as The Tower or Parson's Folly. It is said that the landowner, Mr Parsons of Kemerton Court, made it precisely thirty-nine feet high in order to raise the height of the hill from 961 feet to exactly 1,000 feet, thereby upgrading its status to a mountain. On those not uncommon occasions when it is shrouded in cloud, a local weather-rhyme warns:

'When Bredon Hill puts on his hat
Ye men of the Vale, beware of that.'

In *From A Cotswold Height* (1919), Dr John Henry Garrett, Medical Officer of Health for Cheltenham, described in detail the 'circle of views' and 'wide surrounding outlook' that could be 'obtained' from the top of Broadway Tower. These stretch westward across the rich alluvial plain of the River Severn and Vale of Gloucester to the long granite ridge of the Malvern Hills, and the Black Mountains of Wales beyond; eastward to the red hills marking the borders of Warwickshire, Oxfordshire and Northamptonshire; northward towards Leicestershire and the industrial West Midlands and Shropshire; and southward, where:

> 'the longer view is limited by the high Cotswold country behind Snowshill, including Snowshill Hill.'

Before driving in his automobile up the winding hill, Garrett visited Broadway and wrote of the developing tourist honeypot, and especially of the character of the main street:

> 'This is what I have heard called "Old World". Its air of antiquity is almost unique in its thoroughness. To be appreciated it requires the artistic perception and imagination that recalls the life that has been associated with such appearances, and the desire arises in a few to live that life in that place.'

H J Massingham, however, detested the Worcestershire village – describing it as 'that nucleus of corruption for the countryside' – and went out of his way to avoid it. Indeed, he placed particular emphasis on the fact that 'Broddy' stood at the bottom of Broadway Hill, 'well within the Vale of Evesham' and, therefore, 'technically speaking, it is not Cotswold at all'. In *Wold Without End* (1932), he made his feelings for 'ye olde' village all too clear:

> 'In Broadway you can sing Ancient and Modern at the same time, embracing two worlds and false to both. And Mr Facing-Both-Ways Broadway prospers, and Lot's wife makes a good investment of going forward and looking back. What does it matter if she be turned into a pillar of salt without heart or sensibility or reality of being any more? It pays.'

But, despite its critics, its crowds and its cars, Broadway has a comfortable, cosy, cream-tea charm that appeals to many people, including overseas visitors, especially Americans. Broadway may be billed as the 'Gateway to the Cotswolds', but most foreign tourists enter the region from the east, from London, by way of Oxford, Woodstock and

The Water Terraces, Blenheim Palace

Blenheim Palace, which is the ancestral seat of the Dukes of Marlborough.

Nathaniel Hawthorne (1804–64), the nineteenth-century American novelist, wrote of his impressions of all three places in *Our Old Home: a Series of English Sketches*. With regard to Oxford, he professed to find

Occupying a sheltered and secluded wooded valley, some eight miles south-west of Malmesbury and about a mile east of the Fosse Way, Castle Combe is, in part, named after the Norman castle that stood on the hill to the north (a strategic site also used by the Romans and Anglo-Saxons). 'Combe' refers to the valley of the By Brook. The Wiltshire village was once an important sheep, wool and cloth centre, with a charter that entitled it to hold regular markets and fairs. The Market Cross, sited at the focal point of the settlement, dates from at least the late sixteenth century. It consists of a tilestone and timber roof, supported by four stone pillars, in the centre of which stands a decorated cross. Nearby is a mounting block, known as the Butter Cross. From the Cross, the houses and cottages (once inhabited by clothiers and weavers) descend the hillside to the By Brook, spanned by an old packhorse bridge. The nearby Weaver's House and Weavers' Cottages date from the fifteenth century, when Castle Combe enjoyed the peak of its prosperity.

'no literary faculty, attainable or conceivable' to 'put it adequately, or even tolerably, upon paper. It must remain its own sole expression.' Yet Hawthorne still managed to find some 200 words with which to list the numerous attributes of the university city of Oxford, concluding:

> 'make all these things vivid in your dream, and you will never know nor believe how inadequate is the result to represent even the merest outside of Oxford.'

At Woodstock, Hawthorne and his party stopped for lunch, and to water their horses, at the Black Bear public house:

> 'an ancient inn, large and respectable, with balustraded staircases, and intricate passages and corridors, and queer old pictures and engravings hanging in the entries and apartments.'

Among the many attractions at Blenheim he was particularly struck by High Lodge, the battlemented structure, situated on the far side of the lake to the palace. From the top there is:

> 'a view of the spires of Oxford, and of points much farther off, very indistinctly seen, however, as is usually the case with the misty distances of England . . . Methinks, if such good fortune ever befell a bookish man, I should choose this lodge for my own residence, with the topmost room of the tower for a study, and all the seclusion of cultivated wilderness beneath to ramble in.'

Coincidentally, at the same time as Hawthorne was penning those lines, Broadway Tower was owned by a 'bookish man' – Sir Thomas Phillipps of the nearby Middle Hill house and estate – whose ambition (despite its practical impossibility) was to collect one copy of every book in the world. In the event, before his death in 1872, Phillipps managed to acquire some 60,000 manuscripts and printed books of astonishing diversity: French literature, Welsh and Irish poems, Greek and Latin writings, medieval documents and such precious historical material as letters, charters and deeds.

Since many of his manuscripts had never been published, Phillipps decided to make selected documents more widely available by setting up the Middle Hill Press, which he housed in Broadway Tower. One French scholar, who was invited to Middle Hill for the purpose of research and study, wrote that:

> 'Broadway Tower is like a lighthouse, signalling to the friends of letters that a hospitable roof exists, under which all pilgrims of learning are made welcome.'

In 1863, however, Phillipps decided to move himself and his collection to Cheltenham. The tower was subsequently rented to the Oxford scholar Cormell ('Crom') Price, who, in 1874, became headmaster of the United Services College at Westward Ho!, Devon. Rudyard Kipling attended the colonial boarding school between 1878 and 1882 and dedicated *Stalky & Co.* (1899) to Price, his headmaster (who appeared in the book as Prooshian Bates). During his years at Oxford, Price was part of the 'set' that included Edward Burne-Jones and William Morris, influential figures in the Pre-Raphaelite Brotherhood (though not actually members) and in the Arts and Crafts Movement of the late nineteenth century. Both, together with Dante Gabriel Rossetti, often visited 'Crom's Tower' – 'among the winds and clouds' – using it as a holiday retreat.

It was while staying at the tower in 1876 that Morris wrote a letter to *The Athenaeum*, which led to the formation, in March the following year, of the Society for the Protection of Ancient Buildings, or 'Anti-Scrape' as it was familiarly known. Morris became the Society's honorary secretary and many of its members, such as Burne-Jones, were drawn from his close circle of friends. Part of its public manifesto was an adapted quote from John Ruskin's *The Seven Lamps of Architecture* (1849), a book Morris greatly admired from his Oxford days.

> 'Take proper care of your monuments, and you will not need to restore them. Watch an old building with an anxious care; count its stones as you would jewels of a crown; bind it together with iron where it loosens, stay it with timber where it declines. Do not care about the unsightliness of the aid; better a crutch than a lost limb; and do this tenderly, reverently, continually, and many a generation will still be born to pass away beneath its shadow.'

From 1871 until his death in 1896, aged sixty-two, Morris leased Kelmscott Manor, on the banks of the upper Thames, near Lechlade. In a letter dated 17 May 1871, shortly before he acquired the property, he wrote to his friend and business partner, Charles Faulkner:

> 'Kelmscott, a little village about two miles above Radcott Bridge – a heaven on earth: an old stone Elizabethan house . . . and such a garden! Close down on the river, a boat house and all things handy. I am going down there again on Saturday with Rossetti and my wife: Rossetti because he thinks of sharing it with us if the thing looks likely.'

Rossetti did, in fact, take out a joint tenancy on the house with Morris; but there was a deeper motive than that officially given – to wit, that clean country air was required for the health of Morris's wife, Jane ('Janey'), and their children, all of whom suffered from the effects of living in grimy, soot-blackened London. No – the real reason (which had to be concealed to avoid scandal and social ostracism) was that Rossetti and Janey were having an affair. Since

Despite extensive rebuilding in the traditional style by the owner of Sandford Park (opposite the church) in the mid-nineteenth century, Sandford St Martin contains several older properties, including a long, low, stone-built farmhouse dated 1705 (south of the Old Vicarage). The medieval church, dedicated to St Martin, was restored in the Victorian period by G E Street, who also rebuilt the chancel and erected the lych gate at the entrance to the churchyard. He also added the head to the shaft of the old village cross. The stained glass of 'God inspiring St Martin to share his cloak with the beggar' is by John Piper and Patrick Reyntiens (1973). Sandford Park is essentially eighteenth century, with Victorian additions. The landscaped park (not open to the public) is watered by the River Dorn, a tributary of the Glyme.

neither separation nor divorce was a viable option, Morris had decided, somewhat chivalrously, that – despite his own traumatic feelings of pain, confusion and betrayal – the only solution was to find a shared house deep in the seclusion of the country where at least the veneer of Victorian respectability could be decently maintained.

Morris threw himself into his work: founding and running the Kelmscott Press; managing his business, Morris and Co.; designing textiles and wallpapers; campaigning and lecturing as an early environmentalist, social reformer and educationalist; writing poetry and prose romances; translating Greek and

Icelandic epics; and much more besides. Not surprisingly, while on his deathbed, one of Morris's doctors diagnosed his disease as:

'simply being William Morris, and having done more work than most ten men.'

Despite the staggering amount of time and energy he spent on practical and material activities, particularly with regard to his business, Morris was a romantic dreamer at heart, advocating a return to medieval simplicity and social equality, even if to bring this about meant a total overthrow of the status quo. His Utopian vision of England after the Socialist revolution appeared in the fictional romance *News From Nowhere; or An Epoch of Rest* (1891), on the frontispiece of which was an illustration of Kelmscott Manor, the centre of his earthly paradise. In this dream, or vision, of the future, 'Guest' (Morris) is told:

'This is how we stand. England was once a country of clearings amongst the woods and wastes, with a few towns interspersed, which were fortresses for the feudal army, markets for the folk, gathering places for craftsmen. It then became a country of huge and foul workshops and fouler gambling dens, surrounded by an ill-kept, poverty-stricken farm, pillaged by the masters of the workshops. It is now a garden, where nothing is wasted and nothing is spoilt, with the necessary dwellings, sheds, and workshops scattered up and down the country, all trim and neat and pretty. For, indeed, we should be too much ashamed of ourselves if we allowed the making of goods, even on a large scale, to carry with it the appearance, even, of desolation and misery.'

Central among Morris's Utopian ideas was the belief that the key to social reform lay in a return to medieval craftsmanship, not in the mechanized, mass-production methods that were the Industrial Revolution. The importance he placed on art is emphasized on a printed board in Broadway Tower, headed 'The Dream of William Morris' (its source, unfortunately, is not given):

'That art will make our streets as beautiful as the woods, as elevating as the mountain-sides: it will be a pleasure and a rest, and not a weight upon the spirits to come from the open country into a town; every man's house will be fair and decent, soothing to his mind and helpful to his work: all the works of man that we live among and handle will be in harmony with nature, will be reasonable and beautiful: yet all will be simple and inspiring, not childish and enervating: for as nothing of beauty and splendour that man's mind and hand may compass shall be wanting from our public buildings, so in no private dwelling will there be any signs of waste, pomp, or insolence, and every man will have his share of the best.

It is a dream, you may say, of what has never been and never will be: true, it has never been, and therefore, since the world is alive, and moving yet, my hope is the greater that it one day will be: true it is a dream; but dreams have before now come about of things so good and necessary to us, that we scarcely think of them more than of the daylight, though once people had to live without them, without even the hope of them.'

Many of Morris's theories of craftsmanship and community – in which art, particularly architecture, was created by and for the ordinary working man, as it had been in the Middle Ages – found practical expression in the Arts and Crafts Movement of the late nineteenth and early twentieth centuries; especially among those artists and craftsmen who established workshops in the Cotswolds, notably at Sapperton, Broadway and Chipping Campden. Indeed, for Morris, it was impossible for an artist to exist outside the context of a community. In reality, however, the romantic dream of creating 'art for the people, not for the connoisseur' foundered because craftsmen-built products, especially houses, were too expensive for the ordinary working man to afford.

Among those artists, architects, craftsmen and designers who, under Morris's influence, sought to realize the ideals of the Arts and Crafts Movement by moving to the Cotswolds to live and work, were: Ernest Gimson and the Barnsley brothers (Ernest and Sidney), who set up workshops first at Pinbury and later at Daneway House near Sapperton (they were eventually joined by Norman Jewson, who married one of Ernest Barnsley's daughters); Gordon Russell, whose father, Sydney, bought and renovated the Lygon Arms in the village of Broadway; and Charles Robert Ashbee, who established the Guild of Handicraft at Chipping Campden, and imported some 150 men, women and children from London's East End.

Chipping Campden, at it appeared at the end of the nineteenth century – without cars, without modern road surfaces, without even people – was captured in *The Footpath-Way in Gloucestershire* (1924) by Algernon Gissing ('a cheerful bustling little man', according to Jewson):

'After hours of sunlight on these lonely hills with the skylarks and the plovers, late in the afternoon I saw below me this wide secluded basin, made as it seemed simply to catch the sun, and basking there in the radiance was the little grey town with

curve of what seemed infinite detail and variety yet of matchless harmony. Built all of stone. Turned absolutely to gold just then, this wide street widened still more midway to admit, as islands, the arched pillared and gabled Market Hall and the Gothically buttressed Guildhall. It was indescribable, simply a dream.'

Dover's Hill, situated above Chipping Campden, is celebrated for being the site of Robert Dover's Cotswold 'Olympick' Games, first held in 1612 (although alternative dates have been recorded).

Crimscote Downs and the Feldon, from Ilmington Downs

a majestic church tower shining at one end of it. Gradually I descended into the hollow, and on entering that one wide street, swept by the sun from behind me, I tried to muffle my footsteps in the silence. At the market place I stood in silent astonishment. From end to end nobody was to be seen. My foot alone on the gilded pavement (all consisting then not of cement but of the dove-grey lias stone) had broken the quiet of immemorial sleep and my own sounds only had echoed around me. Between the church tower and the sun lay the antique town in one graceful

They were stopped after the meeting of 1851, when a 'computed' crowd of 30,000 attended. In his introduction to *Cotswold Games: Annalia Dubrensia* (1878), Edward R Vyvyan gave the reason for their termination:

'In later years, from 1846 onwards, the games, instead of being as they originally were intended to be decorously conducted, became the trysting place of all the lowest scum of the population which lived in the districts lying between Birmingham and Oxford. These people came to Dover's Hill and remained there the whole of

Whitsun week, creating all sorts of disturbances, and in short demoralising the whole neighbourhood.'

One of the most popular events of the original games (they were revived in 1951) was shin-kicking,

According to the thirteenth-century chronicler Matthew Paris, Hailes Abbey was founded (in 1246) to fulfil a vow made four years earlier by Richard, Earl of Cornwall, when his life was endangered by a storm at sea. After landing safely, Richard – King of the Romans, son of King John and brother of Henry III – gave thanks by sparing no cost in the erection of a magnificent abbey, sited below the Cotswold escarpment, some three miles north-east of Winchcombe. After the founder's son, Edmund, presented the monks with a phial believed to contain the holy blood of Christ, the Cistercian monastery prospered as an important pilgrimage centre, as well as from the sale of wool. After the abbey's dissolution in 1539 it was stripped of its treasures, including the lead roof, and many of the buildings were demolished for their stone. The remains now belong to the National Trust but are managed by English Heritage.

in which contestant not only fought contestant, but village team fought village team. Rivalry among the north Cotswolds villages – Broadway, Chipping Campden, Willersey, Ebrington, Ilmington and so on – was intense, and contestants went to incredible pains, literally, to achieve success. In the early 1930s, H J Massingham travelled the area:

'fishing among the inns over miles around, for first-hand knowledge of this notable sport.'

At Ebrington, he heard that:

'an old warrior, dead some years, used to sit in the pub and have his shins beaten by a deal plank as a

form of training, while one of the heroes of Campden used to "thrape" his shins with a hammer in order to be deemed worthy of inclusion in the team.'

One stone-breaker from Broadway, apparently, had 'shins that were corrugated like iron'. After the abandonment of the games, however, many of the shin-kickers found alternative 'sport' in challenging men from neighbouring village inns. Other Cotswold 'Olympick' sports, which are now thought cruel and barbaric, but were popular in their day, included cock-fighting, bull-baiting and various forms of hunting. For more gentler souls, there were 'handsome prizes to be danced for', as well as other 'ancient pastimes' such as chess, shovelboard, quoits and skittles.

Dover's Hill is clearly discernible from the top of Broadway Tower. Both are linked by the Cotswold Way, which, unlike most of the island's long-distance footpaths, never strays far from towns and villages. From Chipping Campden – the beginning or end of the 100-mile route – the Way heads south-westward, following, for the most part, the high continuous edge of oolitic escarpment all its length to Bath. There, at Lansdown, on the outskirts of the 'golden city', another monumental folly – Beckford's Tower – offers magnificent views over the south Cotswolds, the valley of the Bristol Avon and to the Bristol Channel beyond.

Interestingly, the 154-foot-high structure was built for William Beckford (1760–1844): the same wealthy author, traveller, collector and eccentric who commissioned James Wyatt to design the neo-Gothic extravaganza Fonthill Abbey. In 1822, after he was forced to sell the abbey because of financial difficulties, Beckford retired to Bath, where he owned two adjacent houses in Lansdown Crescent. Apparently, whenever he went out, he insisted on riding through the streets accompanied by a cavalcade of mounted stewards, a pack of dogs and a dwarf named Perro. The tower, designed in neo-classical Italianate style by a local architect, Henry Goodridge, was built at the top of Beckford's rear garden, which stretched for more than a mile up Lansdown Hill.

Towers of differing sorts can be found throughout the Cotswolds. Many offer bird's-eye views of the surrounding countryside; while others, like those at Oxford and Bath, provide excellent vantage points from which to study the urban landscape. Not all the towers, of course, are follies: a few, such as the Tyndale Monument, on the edge above North Nibley, are commemorative; but most are attached to houses, colleges and churches. Memorable views of Cirencester and its park, for example, can be obtained from the top of the tower of the parish church (unfortunately, access to it is now barred for reasons of public safety).

The tower on top of Broadway Hill, however, is open throughout the tourist season. In addition to serving as a holiday retreat for those connected with Morris and the Pre-Raphaelite Brotherhood, it was used as a place of study by the architect Arthur Evans. From the early years of the twentieth century until 1972 it became a farmhouse, known as Tower Farm. Throughout this period, all of the tenant farmers and their families had to manage without water on tap, proper sewerage facilities, or electricity; nor was the land, with its thin, stony soil, particularly good for cultivation. One enterprising farmer, William Sherratt, supplemented his income by selling postcards of the tower, plus local views, to visitors. The record for the longest tenancy of the farm was held by the Hollingtons, a married couple who lived in the tower for more than forty years, arriving at the beginning of the 1930s.

It was during World War II, on 2 June 1943, that Mr Hollington found himself involved in a dramatic rescue, for which he received a certificate signed by the Prime Minister, Winston Churchill, expressing 'His Majesty's high appreciation of the service rendered'. At the time, Hollington was on duty (together with a Broadway printer, Albert Lowe) as a uniformed member of the Royal Observer Corps – a part-time civilian body set up to report the path of enemy aircraft in the nation's skies. Unfortunately, on the day in question, a Whitley bomber, on a training flight from nearby Honeybourne, in the Vale of Evesham, lost its way in bad weather and crashed into Broadway Hill, only some 650 feet from the tower. Both men rushed to the scene and managed to pull one of the crew from the wreckage of the bomber, but, like the rest of his companions, he died from his injuries.

Although 'Cotswold Lions' can be found at Broadway Tower Country Park and at rare breeds survival centres like the Cotswold Farm Park, near Guiting Power, they are seldom seen grazing the open wolds like other breeds of sheep. Yet, during the Middle Ages, vast flocks of these large-boned, long-woolled animals roamed over the gently swelling hills in almost never-ending waves; their valuable fleeces bringing a golden age to the

From its source on the wolds near Winstone, the six-mile-long Dun Brook runs south-east past the four Duntisbourne settlements to the larger village of Daglingworth, from where it flows to Stratton, before joining the River Churn at Cirencester. The parish church at Daglingworth is one of seven foundations between Stroud and Swindon that have the unusual dedication to the Holy Rood (Holy Cross). Despite being drastically rebuilt in Victorian times, the church preserves elements of Anglo-Saxon work, together with a fifteenth-century west tower and south porch. Daglingworth House, beside the church, dates from the early nineteenth century. In the grounds of the Manor House at Lower End, south of the main village, is a medieval dovecote, complete with revolving ladder. The Roman Ermin Way, or Ermin Street – running from Silchester (near Reading), through Cirencester, to Gloucester – passes just east of Daglingworth and the Duntisbourne valley.

Cotswolds, and immense fortunes for the wool and cloth merchants (as well as monastic institutions), who profited 'upon the backs' of the magnificent creatures. Indeed, apart from the limestone, nothing has shaped the Cotswolds more than wool. Sheep and the Cotswolds have been synonymous for many centuries. As Edith Brill noted in *Life and Tradition on the Cotswolds*:

> 'Even when the wolds became wide arable fields after the Enclosures, sheep were kept on the hills where they fed the land with their manure and

compacted the light soil with their hoofs; the Golden Hoof as well as the Golden Fleece were Cotswold's assets in her golden age.'

In his topographical poem *Poly-Olbion* (1612–22), Michael Drayton described the region as 'that great king of shepherds'. While London-born William

The Lygon Arms, Broadway

Camden, the Elizabethan antiquary and historian, wrote in *Britannia* (1586):

'Upon these hills are fed large flocks of sheep, with the whitest wool, having long necks and square bodies, by reason, as is supposed, of their hilly and short pasture; whose fine wool is much valued in foreign nations.'

Great markets sprang up all over the Cotswolds, bringing huge prosperity to towns such as Chipping Campden, Moreton-in-Marsh, Stow-on-the-Wold, Tetbury and Malmesbury. Increased wealth, in turn, led to the construction of many splendid manors and fine houses, and, more particularly, the building of glorious 'wool' churches, such as those at Northleach, Cirencester and Fairford.

At first the wool was exported raw to Europe, where it was manufactured into cloth. Sensing that even greater profits could be made by producing the finished product in England, the wool merchants, and others, including the Crown, began to encourage local people to spin and weave the wool in their own homes. In turn, the woven wool was taken to fulling mills (owned by the clothiers), where it was shrunk and thickened into cloth. Since deposits of fuller's earth – a yellow clay used in the process of cleansing

and felting cloth – occurred naturally around Stroud and Minchinhampton, the district became a major centre of the Cotswold cloth industry. Another important factor in the industrial development of the area was the availability of abundant supplies of pure, soft, fast-flowing water for washing and dyeing the cloth and powering the mills. Indeed, so much wealth was generated for the clothiers in the five valleys that converge on Stroud – Painswick, Slad, Chalford, Toadsmoor and Nailsworth – that they came to be known as the 'Golden Valleys'.

The largest, the Chalford valley, is watered by the River Frome: one of only three main rivers to rise on the limestone plateau and flow west into the Severn (the others are the Little Avon and the Bristol Avon). Most Cotswold rivers, however, flow south and east to join the Thames; foremost among these are the Evenlode, Windrush, Leach, Coln and Churn. Few flow north and west into the Warwickshire Avon and the Stour. Among the countless minor streams that feed the major rivers is the Badsey Brook, the headwaters of which rise on the steep escarpment above Broadway, near Snowshill and Broadway Hill. After flowing north-west across the Vale of Evesham, it enters the Warwickshire Avon near Evesham.

Some of the region's rivers and streams lend their names to towns and villages lying along their course: Evenlode, Ampney St Mary, Ampney St Peter, Coln Rogers, Coln St Dennis, Coln St Aldwyns, Duntisbourne Rouse, Duntisbourne Leer, Duntisbourne Abbots, Northleach, Eastleach Martin and Eastleach Turville, to cite the more obvious examples. The longest of the truly Cotswold rivers is the Windrush, yet it covers only thirty miles from source to Thames. The latter, however, is probably the region's most celebrated river, rising as it does on the limestone hills near Cirencester, before flowing south-westward to Oxford (where it is known as the 'Isis'), London and the North Sea.

Indeed, when Daniel Defoe travelled over the wolds in the early eighteenth century, he found the Thames usurping the name of several Cotswold rivers. In *A Tour Thro' the Whole Island of Great Britain* (1724–26) he wrote:

'In passing this way we very remarkably crossed four rivers within the length of about 10 miles, and enquiring their names, the country people called them every one the Thames, which moved me a little to enquire the reason, which is no more than this; namely, that these rivers, which are, the Lech, the Coln, the Churn, and the Isis; all rising in the Cotswolds Hills and joining together and making a full stream at Lechlade, near this place, they become one river there, and are called Thames, or vulgarly Temms.'

Although the official source of the Thames is at Thames Head, south-west of Cirencester, there are some who claim that its real source is that of the Churn, which rises, further away, at Seven Springs, high on the escarpment above Cheltenham.

Cotswold rivers and streams – clear, sparkling, trout-frequented and secretive for much of their journeys – are an integral part of the Cotswold landscape. In his classic book about the region's countryside, *A Cotswold Village* (1898), J Arthur Gibbs wrote (after reflecting on a 'cold and uninviting' trout stream in the dead of winter):

'But the delight of a clear stream is found in the spring and summer; then those cool, shaded deeps and sparkling eddies please us by their contrast to the hot, burning sun; and we love, even if we are not fishermen, to linger by the bank 'neath the shade of ash and beech and alder, and watch the wonderful life around us in the water and in the air.'

Strangely, despite all its celebrated qualities of scenic and architectural beauty, harmony and enchantment, the Cotswolds (Oxford excluded, since it is not technically part of the region) boasts few writers or poets of national, let alone international, distinction. Many famous names have lived in or travelled through the region. Some, even, have been inspired to put pen to paper and produce acclaimed classics: possibly the best known being Edward Thomas's poem *Adlestrop*, written after his train made an unscheduled stop at the Cotswold village whilst he was travelling to Leddington, near Ledbury, in 1914. John Masefield, John Keble, Alexander Pope, A E Housman, J M Barrie, Mrs Delany (Mary Granville) and the Mitford sisters (Jessica and Nancy), all are associated with the area to a greater of lesser extent. But, apart from William Morris, it is probably Laurie Lee who first springs to mind when the names of Cotswold poets and writers are mentioned.

Lee's best-known work was *Cider With Rosie*, which was first published in 1959. In it he gave a wonderfully evocative account of his boyhood in the Slad valley, near Stroud, during and after World War I. Many years later, when his 'pastoral paradise' was threatened by a new housing estate, he wrote in the *Daily Mail* (Saturday, 1 April 1995):

'It was in these meadows where I breathed the first faint musks of sex and where Rosie Burdock shared her cider with me during haymaking, on a motionless day of summer, hazy and amber-coloured, with the beech trees standing in heavy sunlight as though clogged with wild, wet honey – a day when the hay wagon under which we lay went floating away like a barge out over the valley.'

Like Laurie Lee, numerous poets and writers have drawn inspiration from memories of childhood and the comforting image of rural England in a golden age; an age that vaguely existed sometime before the outbreak of World War I; sometime before the widespread introduction of cars, concrete and computers. The irretrievable loss of this vague and visionary 'remembered' country was lamented by the poet A E Housman in *A Shropshire Lad* (1896).

'That is the land of lost content,
I see it shining plain.
The happy highways where I went
And cannot come again.'

From Broadway Tower it is also possible to look out across Housman's 'coloured counties' to the 'blue remembered hills' of Shropshire. Sadly, there are those who treat with disdain any poetic vision of England that is at variance with the reality. There are others, however, who find it impossible not to dream; impossible not to imagine, like William Morris, an 'earthly paradise', where 'our streets' are 'as beautiful as the woods, as elevating as the mountain-sides.'

How else, except through dreams, can such visionaries experience that enlargement of imagination that stretches beyond the limits of self, beyond the limits of earth and sky to embrace the stars?

And, for those 'dreamers of dreams', the fresh, invigorating, wind-swept summit of Broadway Hill is an idyllic spot on which to pause and let the golden magic and timeless mystery of the Cotswold landscape weave its unique and captivating spell.

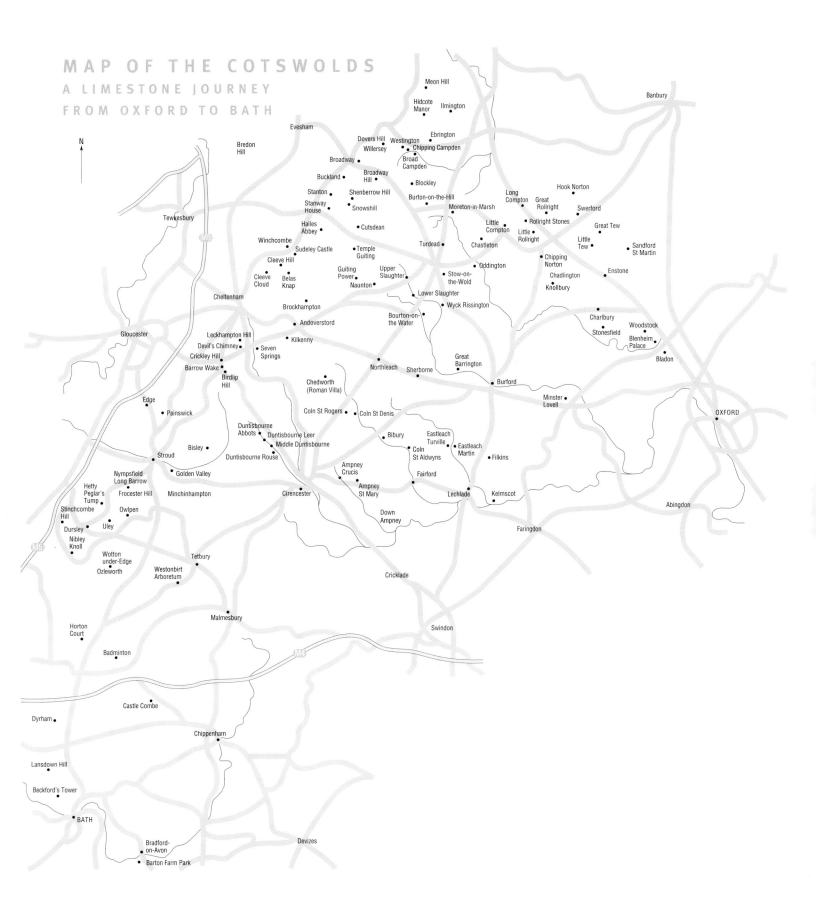

MAP OF THE COTSWOLDS
A LIMESTONE JOURNEY
FROM OXFORD TO BATH

N

Meon Hill
Banbury
Hidcote Manor
Ilmington
Evesham
Bredon Hill
Dovers Hill
Westington
Ebrington
Willersey
Chipping Campden
Broadway
Broad Campden
Buckland
Broadway Hill
Blockley
Hook Norton
Stanton
Shenberrow Hill
Burton-on-the-Hill
Long Compton
Great Rollright
Swerford
Stanway House
Snowshill
Moreton-in-Marsh
Tewkesbury
Rollright Stones
Great Tew
Hailes Abbey
Cutsdean
Little Compton
Little Rollright
Little Tew
Winchcombe
Temple Guiting
Turdead
Chastleton
Sandford St Martin
Sudeley Castle
Cleeve Hill
Oddington
Chipping Norton
Cleeve Cloud
Belas Knap
Guiting Power
Upper Slaughter
Stow-on-the-Wold
Chadlington
Knollbury
Enstone
Cheltenham
Naunton
Lower Slaughter
Brockhampton
Wyck Rissington
Charlbury
Woodstock
Bourton-on-the Water
Stonesfield
Blenheim Palace
Gloucester
Andoverstord
Bladon
Leckhampton Hill
Kilkenny
Great Barrington
Devil's Chimney
Seven Springs
Northleach
Sherborne
Burford
Crickley Hill
Barrow Wake
Minster Lovell
Birdlip Hill
Chedworth (Roman Villa)
OXFORD
Edge
Coln St Rogers
Coln St Denis
Painswick
Duntisbourne Abbots
Bibury
Eastleach Turville
Duntisbourne Leer
Eastleach Martin
Bisley
Middle Duntisbourne
Coln St Aldwyns
Filkins
Stroud
Duntisbourne Rouse
Fairford
Nympsfield Long Barrow
Golden Valley
Ampney Crucis
Lechlade
Kelmscot
Hetty Peglar's Tump
Frocester Hill
Minchinhampton
Cirencester
Ampney St Mary
Abingdon
Stinchcombe Hill
Owlpen
Down Ampney
Faringdon
Dursley
Uley
Nibley Knoll
Wotton under-Edge
Tetbury
Ozleworth
Westonbirt Arboretum
Cricklade
Horton Court
Swindon
Malmesbury
Badminton
Castle Combe
Dyrham
Chippenham
Lansdown Hill
Beckford's Tower
BATH
Bradford-on-Avon
Devizes
Barton Farm Park

OXFORD

'And that sweet city with her dreaming spires,

She needs not June for beauty's heightening.'

MATTHEW ARNOLD, *THYRSIS* (1867)

All the oolitic limestone used to build the medieval city of Oxford – sited just north of the confluence of the River Thames (Isis) and its tributary the Cherwell – came from the Cotswolds, especially from the Burford area. Quarried in the valley of the Windrush, another tributary of the Thames, the cut stone was transported downstream to the university city, and even to London. Indeed, after the Great Fire of 1666, the architect Christopher Wren used Burford stone for rebuilding many of London's churches, including St Paul's Cathedral. Among the buildings at Oxford designed by Wren are: the Sheldonian Theatre (his first architectural commission) and the upper part of Tom Tower at Christ Church. He is also credited with designing the great sundial at All Souls. The evolution of the market town into the site of Britain's first university began during the reign of Henry II, when English scholars in Europe, particularly Paris, were forced to return home. Although University College, founded in 1249, is the earliest surviving college, it was Merton, founded in 1264, that set the pattern adopted as the standard by many later foundations. From the tower of the university church of St Mary the Virgin there are excellent views over the city, including the Bodleian Library, founded by Thomas Bodley and officially opened in 1602, and the domed Radcliffe Camera (now part of the Bodleian), built between 1737 and 1749 as an independent library by James Gibbs with money bequeathed by Dr John Radcliffe. Magdalen College, founded in 1458, has its own river walk and deer park. Christ Church, standing on the site of an Anglo-Saxon monastery and medieval priory, was founded as a cathedral and a college by Henry VIII in 1546. Its bell, 'Great Tom', in the Tom Tower, tolls 101 times at 9.05 each evening, signifying the number of original scholars, plus one added later.

The Bodleian Library,

Radcliffe Camera and

St Mary's Church, Oxford

The Hall and Bodley
Tower, Christ Church
College, Oxford

Sheldonian Theatre, Oxford

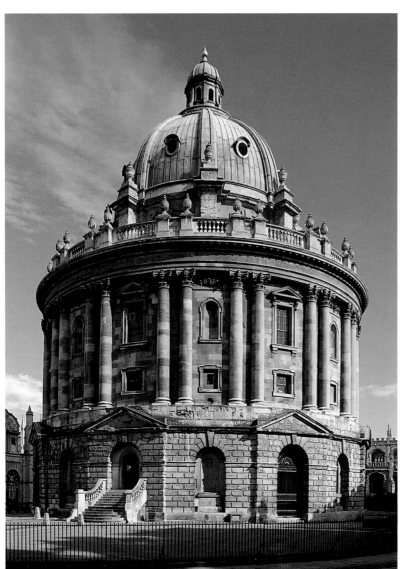

Radcliffe Camera, Oxford

Meadow Cottages and
Magdalen College
Bell-Tower, Oxford

Ancestral home of the Dukes of Marlborough and birthplace of Sir Winston Churchill, Blenheim Palace, set in more than 2,000 acres of 'Capability' Brown parkland, was designed as a national monument by John Vanbrugh for John Churchill, 1st Duke of Marlborough. The palace, considered to be one of the finest examples of English Baroque architecture, was built to commemorate the Duke's decisive victory over the French in 1704 at the battle of Blindheim (Blenheim) in Bavaria. Although the inscription on the East Gate states that 'this Royal Manor of Woodstock, together with a grant of £240,000, towards the building of Blenheim was given by Her Majesty Queen Anne and confirmed by Act of Parliament',

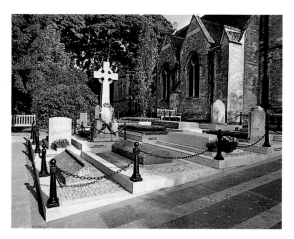

The Churchill graves, St Martin's Churchyard, Bladon

The Great Court

the terms and amount of funds were never specified in any kind of document. In 1710, the Duchess fell out with the Queen and two years later the Marlboroughs went into 'a sort of exile'. Following their return in 1714 (after the death of the Queen), the Duke completed the palace at his own expense. Although Vanbrugh (assisted by Nicholas Hawksmoor) resumed work on the building, both

The Column of Victory

men left after the Duchess took over supervision from the Duke in 1716. Building continued thereafter under James Moore, a cabinet-maker, and Vanbrugh never returned. Hawksmoor, however, was recalled after the Duke's death in 1722 and completed various rooms and outbuildings, including the Triumphal Arch. The Column of Victory, surmounted by a lead statue of the Duke, was completed in 1730. The Water Terraces, constructed between 1925 and 1930, were designed for the 9th Duke by Achille Duchêne, who also designed the Italian Garden. In 1895, Lord Randolph Churchill, second son of the 7th Duke of Marlborough and father of Sir Winston, was the first member of the family to be buried at nearby Bladon. Sir Winston was buried there in 1965.

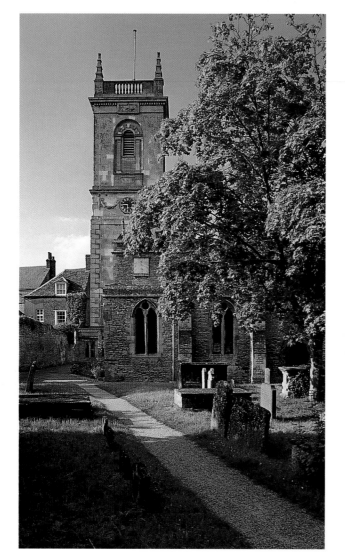

On the north-east edge of Blenheim Park and some seven miles north-west of Oxford, the former market town of Woodstock – once famed for the manufacture of gloves – was the site of a royal residence during Anglo-Saxon times. The name 'Woodstock' is derived from the Old English for 'a place in the wood'. After the Norman Conquest, Henry I built a new manor house on the site. He also enclosed the royal park with a stone wall some seven miles in circumference, stocking it with camels, leopards, lions and other wild animals, including a porcupine. The royal residence, subsequently rebuilt and enlarged, eventually fell into ruin and was demolished during the construction of Blenheim Palace in the early eighteenth century. The first settlement that grew up outside the walls of the royal park was Old Woodstock, on the hillside above the River Glyme. New Woodstock, found on the opposite side of the river, dates from the late twelfth century, when Henry II granted it a market charter.

Park Street, Woodstock

Legend says that Henry's mistress, Rosamond Clifford ('Fair Rosamond'), was murdered at Woodstock by his jealous wife, Queen Eleanor. Most houses of the present town are seventeenth or eighteenth century. The medieval church of St Mary Magdalene, formerly a chapel of Bladon church, was essentially rebuilt in 1878. Its tower is late eighteenth century. Chaucer's House, in Park Street, stands on the site of a property reputedly owned by Geoffrey Chaucer's son Thomas, a wealthy merchant and Speaker of the House of Commons, who died in 1434.

29

Oolitic limestone, the underlying rock predominating in the Cotswolds, is composed of rounded granules of lime that resemble the roe of fish (hence its alternative name of eggstone). Dating from the Jurassic period, more than 140 million years ago (when what was to become the Cotswolds not only lay beneath a warm, shallow sea, but was also situated much further south, nearer the equator), the granules were gradually transformed into limestone rock by enormous pressures due to changes and movements in the Earth's crust. Limestone makes excellent building material. Quarried locally, the stone is easy to work when first removed from the ground, but it gradually hardens when exposed to the air until it is able to withstand centuries of weathering. Its colour, ranging from

Drystone wall, Snowshill

30

*Dovecote on garage,
Blockley*

*Tilestone roof,
Duntisbourne Rouse*

silver-grey to golden-brown, varies from area to area within the region. Since far distant times, the stone has been fashioned into an infinite variety of structures: from prehistoric burial mounds to medieval churches; from functional dovecotes to mansions; and from drystone walls to castle ramparts. The roofs of traditional Cotswold buildings – whether manor or barn – are constructed with tilestones (a sandy limestone that easily splits into thin layers). These stone roofing slates are pegged on the timber framework in graduated courses: the largest at the eaves and the smallest at the ridge. The characteristic, often attractive, undulating roof found on old and neglected properties is simply caused by the supporting timbers sagging under the weight of the stone.

On a prominent hilltop site overlooking the Evenlode valley, midway between Woodstock and Charlbury, stands the Oxfordshire village of Stonesfield, with its manor, church, cottages, inns and tiny lock-up. In *Cotswold Country* (1937) Massingham considered 'the setting of the large grey, masculine, ridge-cold village' to be 'one of the finest in the eastern Cotswolds'. Stonesfield slate (Jurassic limestone that can be readily split by frost when first

exposed to air) was extensively mined in the locality from the sixteenth century until the early twentieth century. This high-quality stone was used as the roofing material for countless Cotswold houses, barns and churches, including many colleges and buildings in Oxford. The commemorative slate, or tilestone, in the church came from the old rectory (now known as Stonesfield Manor), built *c.*1650.

Stonesfield

Knollbury, near Chadlington

Knollbury – which is located on rising ground above the village of Chadlington, almost three miles south of Chipping Norton – is a prehistoric burial mound, scheduled as an ancient monument. The grasses and wild flowers, which have been encouraged to grow on its banks, attract summer grassland butterflies such as the marbled white, small heath, meadow brown and common blue. The Hawk Stone, one and a half miles to the east, is an eight-feet-high standing stone that is thought to date from the Bronze Age. Sir Henry Creswicke Rawlinson, the Assyriologist and political agent, was born at nearby Chadlington Manor in 1810. One of his most celebrated achievements was to decipher the cuneiform inscriptions of Darius the Great, King of Persia, which were written on a rock face at Behistun (in present-day Iran) in the sixth century BC. He was created a baronet in 1891.

At 650 feet above sea-level, the old woollen and market centre of Chipping Norton is the highest town in Oxfordshire. 'Chipping' is derived from the Old English *caepen*, meaning 'market place'; 'Norton', of course, means 'north town'. The great 'wool' church of St Mary, built in the Perpendicular style, stands testimony to the town's prosperity in the fifteenth century. The earliest parts of the church, however, date from the twelfth century, while the tower was rebuilt in the 1820s. Among the memorial brasses inside the church are those of two wealthy wool merchants – John Yonge and John Stokes – both dating from the mid-fifteenth century. In 1549, the vicar of Chipping Norton, Henry Joyce, was hanged from the tower for being among the leaders of a local revolt against the replacement of the established Latin service books with the first English Book of Common Prayer. Immediately north of the church are the earthwork remains of a Norman motte-and-bailey castle. The gabled almshouses, in Church Street, were built by Henry Cornish in 1640. Originally there were eight houses (with nine chimneys), but they have now been converted into four larger dwellings. In the valley, on the western outskirts of the town, is the imposing Bliss Tweed Mill, built of Cotswold stone in 1872 after the earlier building had been destroyed by fire (caused by an exploding boiler). Despite having a prominent central chimney, the mill-owner, William Bliss, wanted the building to resemble a country mansion set in a park. The architect employed to undertake the work was George Woodhouse from Lancashire, who specialized in designing mills and factories. The building, once linked by rail to the main line owned by the Oxford, Worcester and Wolverhampton Railway Company (OWWR), has now been converted into private apartments.

Bliss (Tweed) Mill, Chipping Norton

Henry Cornish almshouses, Chipping Norton

There are three Oxfordshire Tews: two (Great and Little Tew) lie close to each other, five miles east of Chipping Norton; the third (Duns Tew) is several miles further east. At one time they were all part of the same parish. The largest, Great Tew, is celebrated for its idyllic setting – with thatched ironstone cottages, post office and Falkland Arms inn facing the school and a sloping green. The thirteenth- and fourteenth-century church of St Michael and All Angels contains fragments of an earlier Norman foundation and stands on a hill at the edge of Great Tew Park, south of the village. Inside is a monument to Lucius Cary, Lord Falkland, who was Secretary of State to Charles I and who was killed at the battle of Newbury in 1643. His manor house was demolished in the early nineteenth century and now only the stables, dovecote and garden walls remain. It was replaced by a new manor, nearer the village. Much of Great Tew's 'picturesque' appearance is due to the landscaping skills of John Claudius Loudon, the Scottish architect and agriculturalist, who managed the estate for G F Stratton between 1809 and 1811. Matthew Robinson Boulton (the son of Matthew Boulton of Birmingham, considered by some to be the 'Father of the Industrial Revolution') was responsible for embellishing or rebuilding many of the cottages, as well as for constructing a new link road to the Square. Further rebuilding, including the construction of a new school and significant changes to the existing road system, was carried out by his son, M P W Boulton.

The Falkland Arms,
Great Tew

Cottage by the Square,

Great Tew

Church and cottages,

Little Tew

37

Two miles south-east of Hook Norton, near the head of the Swere valley (a tributary of the Cherwell), is the little village of Swerford. The village occupies sloping ground at the edge of Swerford Park – the house of which dates from the eighteenth century, but was remodelled in the 1820s by J M Gandy, who was once an assistant of the architect Sir John Soane. St Mary's church, situated by the village green, is traditionally believed to have been built with stone that was taken from the Norman castle, which was demolished on the orders of Henry II. Although the earthwork remains of a motte-and-bailey castle dating from Norman times can be traced near the church, little is known about its history. The earliest part of St Mary's – significantly altered in the Victorian period – is the west tower, which is capped by a small broach-spire, dating from the late thirteenth or early fourteenth century.

Swerford

Netting Street, Hook Norton

Most of the houses and cottages in the hillside village of Hook Norton are built of local rusty coloured ironstone, including the oldest parts of the parish church of St Mary, dating from Norman times. Its pinnacled Perpendicular tower, however, is of a different stone. Among the items of interest in the church, which include an eighteenth-century 'fire engine' and fragments of medieval wall paintings, is a remarkable Norman font carved with figures depicting Adam and Eve and certain signs of the zodiac. The symbolism is said to represent the triumph of good over evil. At the western end of the village is a Victorian brewery (still in operation), while to the east are the massive piers of a dismantled railway viaduct (over which trucks once carried locally quarried ironstone).

Little Rollright

Rollright Stones

Set high on a ridge, straddling the Oxfordshire-Warwickshire border and within the triangle formed by the neighbouring settlements of Great Rollright, Little Rollright and Long Compton, the Rollright Stones consist of a stone circle, a nearby standing stone and, a quarter of a mile away, a group of five stones (the exposed remains of a burial chamber). Dating from prehistoric times, more than 3,500 years ago, the stones – which have been eroded into strange contorted shapes – are surrounded by mystery and legend. One tradition says that an invading king and his army met a witch just below the crest of the ridge above Long Compton. After enquiring about the outcome of his attempt to conquer England, the witch pointed to the top of the ridge and said: 'Seven long strides thou shalt take, and, / If Long Compton thou canst see, / King of England thou shalt be.' Confident that success was assured, the king strode forth, only to find that his view of the village from the top of the ridge was obscured by a long mound of earth. Cackling with delight, the witch turned the king and his men to stone with these words: 'As Long Compton thou canst not see, / King of England thou shalt not be. / Rise up, stick, and stand still, stone, / For King of England thou shalt be none, / Thou and thy men hoar stones shall be, / And I myself an eldern tree.' The stone circle is known as the 'King's Men', the single monolith the 'King Stone' and the distant stones the 'Whispering Knights'. The latter are said to have been petrified while lingering behind to plot treason. It is said that one day the spell will be broken and the king will finally achieve his ambition to rule England.

The Warwickshire villages of Long and Little Compton lie close to the Oxfordshire border, some four or five miles eastward of Moreton-in-Marsh. The larger, Long Compton – strung out along the main road below the long ridge occupied by the Rollright Stones – was once notorious for witchcraft. Local belief in the power of witches continued until well into the twentieth century. In 1875, a Long Compton man slew one old woman with his sickle because he was convinced that she had caused the debilitating pains and cramps in his legs. At his trial he accused a further sixteen women in the village of being witches and of causing all manner of misfortunes, including the death of horses and cattle. Although found guilty of murder, he was declared insane and incarcerated, rather than hanged. Nevertheless, convinced that the witches were trying to 'get inside him', he refused to eat and drink and soon died. The approach to the parish church of St Peter and St Paul is through an unusual lych gate, consisting of a seventeenth-century 'cottage' on 'stilts'. Tradition says that in the sixth century St Augustine visited the Anglo-Saxon church at Long Compton and raised a man from his grave. From the eleventh to the fifteenth centuries, the manor and church at neighbouring Little Compton – once known as Compton-in-Floribus (Compton-in-the-Flowers) – belonged to Deerhurst Priory. Today the manorial buildings (dating from the sixteenth century and remodelled in the seventeenth) are occupied by Reed College. The medieval church of St Denys was destroyed in the 1860s (except for the fourteenth-century saddleback tower) and rebuilt using some of the old materials.

Church and Manor (Reed College), Little Compton

Lych gate and church, Long Compton

St Mary's Church and
Chastleton House

Chastleton House

Hidden in a fold of the Oxfordshire hills, six miles north-east of Stow-on-the-Wold, Chastleton House is one of the finest and least altered Jacobean houses in England. The name 'Chastleton' may be derived from the Old English words for 'fortified camp' and 'town'; the former possibly referring to the Iron Age hillfort above the village. The historic property (now in the care of the National Trust) was built in the early seventeenth century by Walter Jones, a wealthy lawyer, who purchased the estate from Robert Catesby (one of the conspirators in the Gunpowder Plot to blow up Parliament). The fact that the building managed to survive almost unspoiled in its original form was due to Jones's descendants having neither the inclination nor the money to update its architectural style.

It was at Chastleton in 1865 that Walter Jones-Whitmore formulated the rules of croquet, which were officially adopted three years later. Tradition has it that in 1651 his ancestor, Arthur Jones 'the Cavalier' – pursued by Parliamentarian forces after the battle of Worcester – hid in a small 'secret' room at Chastleton. After finding his exhausted horse in the stables, Cromwell's soldiers decided to search the house. But first they demanded food and drink from Jones's wife, Sarah, and somewhere to sleep for the night. Unfortunately, the room where they decided to retire led directly to the fugitive's hiding place. Sarah, however, managed to drug their drink and while the soldiers slept, her husband tiptoed out through the room and made good his escape.

Three miles east of Stow-on-the-Wold, the village of Oddington grew up on the west bank of the River Evenlode, near the medieval church of St Nicholas. In the early eighteenth century, the settlement was abandoned – possibly because of plague – and rebuilt higher up the hillside. In 1852, a new parish church was erected at Upper Oddington and by the end of the century the church of St Nicholas at Lower Oddington stood derelict – the roof open to the sky, the windows broken and the exterior walls matted with ivy. Its restoration began in 1912. Removal of the whitewash that had covered the interior walls since at least the mid-seventeenth century revealed a remarkable series of wall paintings, including the fourteenth-century 'Doom' or 'Last Judgement'. Despite these gruesome scenes, however, the atmosphere inside is warm and memorable.

St Nicholas Church, Lower Oddington

At some 800 feet above sea-level, Stow-on-the-Wold is the highest town in the Cotswolds. Situated between the valleys of the Dikler and Evenlode, it stands at the intersection of eight main roads, the most important being the Roman Fosse Way, running north from Bath, through Cirencester, to Leicester and beyond. From pre-historic origins, when the hilltop site was occupied by Neolithic settlers, Stow developed into a major market town, receiving its first royal charter at the beginning of the twelfth century. In the Domesday Book of 1086, the settlement was known as Edwardstow. Although a carved representation of St Edward the Confessor appears on the head of the market cross (restored in both 1878 and 1995), the town's patron saint may, alternatively, have been Edward the Martyr, or possibly a local hermit, who gave his name to a spring or well on Stow Hill. In *A New*

History of Gloucestershire (1779) Samuel Rudder wrote: 'It is commonly said, that Stow wants three elements out of four. It wants water, from its high situation, and having little or no land belonging to the town, and consequently no produce or fuel, it is deficient in earth and fire: but it has air enough, which in this mountainous and exposed situation, must necessarily be very sharp and piercing, tho' pure, and perhaps, for strong constitutions, healthy.' Despite being known as a place 'where the wind blows cold', Stow attracts many visitors to its shops, inns, narrow streets and large market square, including traders attending its twice-yearly fairs. The church of St Edward was used as a prison for more than 1,000 Royalists captured after the Civil War battle near Stow in 1646.

Market Cross and The King's Arms, Stow-on-the-Wold

Church Street, Stow-on-the-Wold

S ituated at the intersection of two major routes – the Fosse Way and the main road from Oxford to Worcester – Moreton-in-Marsh has its origins in the first century AD, when the Romans established a military camp about half a mile from the town centre. Its development as a major market town dates from the thirteenth century, when the lord of the manor, the Abbot of Westminster,

Mann Institute,
Moreton-in-Marsh

was granted a charter to hold a weekly market, and later a yearly fair. The town hall (or Redesdale Hall) is thought to stand on the site of the earlier market hall, described by Rudder in 1779 as 'a public building upon pillars'. The present hall was built with stone from the quarries at Bourton-on-the-Hill in 1887 by Algernon Bertram Freeman-Mitford (later 1st Lord Redesdale) of nearby

Parish church, Moreton-in-Marsh

Batsford Park. His son, David Freeman-Mitford, 2nd Lord Redesdale, fathered the six 'Mitford Girls', including Nancy, the novelist, Diana, the wife of Oswald Mosley, and Unity, a close friend of Adolf Hitler. The Curfew Tower, abutting the building opposite the town hall, dates from the sixteenth century and was once used as a lock-up. Behind it stands the Mann Institute, erected as a working men's club in 1891 by Edith Mann, daughter of John Mann, the Congregational Minister. St David's parish church, with its 116-feet-high spire, also dates from the Victorian period. During medieval times the town was known as 'Moreton Henmarsh', a name thought to derive from the fact that the surrounding land was boggy and populated by moorhens.

Located midway between the Sezincote estate and Batsford Park, two miles due west of Moreton-in-Marsh, Bourton-on-the-Hill is a pleasant village, marred by traffic thundering up and down its steep, east-facing main street (along which it developed in the seventeenth century). At the bottom of the hill stands Bourton House, dating from the sixteenth century and rebuilt in the early eighteenth century. The gabled Cotswold stone barn of one of the village's two manor houses bears the date 1570. During the seventeenth century, the house was owned by Sir Thomas Overbury. His uncle, another Sir Thomas (1581–1613), was murdered by slow poisoning in the Tower of London – the discovery of which led to a great scandal involving Frances Howard, Countess of Essex, and Robert Carr (later Earl of Somerset), the favourite of James I. It was the Bourton Sir Thomas who wrote the first account of 'The Campden Wonder' in 1676 (*see Broadway Hill, pp. 66–7*). At the top of Bourton's hill stands the eighteenth-century Horse and Groom inn and, beyond, the village's second manor house, rebuilt in the eighteenth century. Centre stage, in the middle of the hill, stands the parish church of St Laurence, dating from Norman times, but much altered over the succeeding centuries. 'Sundial Cottage', opposite the church, forms part of an attractive terrace of seventeenth- and eighteenth-century houses, with front gardens that step steeply up the main road like giant stone window-boxes.

Church and cottages, Bourton-on-the-Hill   *Bourton-on-the-Hill*

Blockley

The old industrial village of Blockley, midway between Moreton-in-Marsh and Chipping Campden, occupies a steep hillside position with narrow lanes dropping precipitously down into the valley of the Blockley Brook. The fast-flowing stream, a tributary of the Knee Brook and River Stour, has long been used as a source of power. The Domesday Book of 1086 records no fewer than twelve mills in the village, all owned by the Bishop of Worcester. In the late eighteenth and early nineteenth centuries, Blockley mills were not only preparing silk for the ribbon-making factories of Coventry, they were also used for grinding corn, fulling cloth, making cider and manufacturing paper. There was also a piano factory and an iron foundry in the village. Today, most of the old mills have been converted into private dwellings, with the running stream forming a central feature of their gardens. Joanna Southcott, the prophetess – who was consulted by many rich and famous people, including the Prince Regent (later George IV) – reputedly lived at Rock Cottage from 1804 until her death in 1814. The whereabouts of the 'Great Box', in which some of her predictions were sealed, remains a mystery.

St Eadburgha's
Churchyard, Ebrington
Stoke Hill, near
Ebrington Hill

Rivalry between the Gloucestershire village of Ebrington and its Warwickshire neighbour, Ilmington, led to the inhabitants of the latter spreading countless tales about the stupidity of the 'Yubberton mawms'. According to one such story, the Ebrington folk tried to make the church tower grow by spreading a pile of manure around its base. Despite the fact that the muck had sunk overnight through heavy rain, the villagers swore that the tower had grown several inches. After a while, when the tower seemed incapable of further growth, the parson suggested pushing it higher up the hill. As a yardstick, to measure their success in performing the task, several of the inhabitants took off their coats and put them down on the far side of the tower. While everybody was pushing and heaving against the wall of the building, two passing strangers saw the coats and stole off with them, unseen. Inevitably, when the men eventually stopped heaving and went round to the far side of the tower, they were convinced that they had pushed so hard that the structure had gone over their coats. On their way to the pub to celebrate their achievement, they all remarked how much higher and grander the tower now looked.

Woodmeadow Farm, Ilmington Downs

Darlingscott and Stour Valley, from Windmill Hill

Ilmington

At the northernmost tip of the Cotswolds, below Windmill Hill and the high undulating downs, the brick- and stone-built Warwickshire village of Ilmington clusters around the church of St Mary and along the slopes of a banked village green. To the north and east lies the Feldon, or 'field-land' – the rich agricultural claylands of south Warwickshire and the lower Stour valley. Although the Feldon was an important corn-growing area in the medieval period, many landowners converted the fields into sheep and cattle pastures during the fifteenth and sixteenth centuries. The highest point in Warwickshire reaches 854 feet on the downs above the village. Inside the church, dating from Norman times, are carved-oak furnishings, installed in the 1930s by Robert Thompson of Kilburn, North Yorkshire. His trademark, a carved mouse, can be found in eleven places. The church and churchyard are reputedly haunted by the ghost of Edmund Golding, a former parish clerk who died in 1793. In 1934, from the gabled Elizabethan house, Ilmington Manor, George V made the first royal Christmas broadcast to the nation. Traditional dancing by the Ilmington Morris Men is performed on certain days of the year, including Garden Day, when some of the villagers open their gardens for inspection by the public.

The Old Garden, Hidcote Manor Garden

On the western slopes of Ilmington Downs, four miles north-east of Chipping Campden, Hidcote Manor boasts one of the most celebrated gardens to be found in all England – the innovatory layout and planting of which has influenced millions of gardeners throughout the world. In 1907, when Lawrence Waterbury Johnston acquired the late-seventeenth-century manor house, its tiny hamlet of thatched cottages (Hidcote Bartrim) and nearly 300 acres of land, there was no garden. Instead, there were only a few specimen trees and an extensive view over the Vale of Evesham to Bredon Hill and beyond. Almost immediately, without any real experience as a plantsman, the Paris-born soldier and farmer set about transforming the bare, windswept area of uncultivated hillside – some 600 feet above sea-level – into a garden. The theme of the development was a series of distinctive outdoor 'rooms', which was an entirely original and inno-vative idea at that time. For seven years (before he went off

Cottages, Hidcote Bartrim

The Pillar Garden, Hidcote Manor Garden

to fight in World War I as a Major in the Northumberland Fusiliers) Johnston laboured – planning, digging and planting – until the basic shape and structure of the ten-acre garden had been properly established. In 1948, after signing over Hidcote to the National Trust, Johnston left Britain to live almost entirely in France. A lifelong bachelor, he died in 1958 and was buried beside his mother in Mickleton churchyard, only a mile west of his renowned creation at Hidcote.

The most northerly point of the Cotswolds, six miles south of Stratford-upon-Avon, is Meon Hill. It is topped by the earthwork remains of an Iron Age hillfort and overlooks the Vale of Evesham, the village of Mickleton and, at its foot, the settlements of Upper and Lower Quinton. Legend says that the 636-feet-high hill was created by the Devil, who threw a huge rock at Evesham Abbey from Ilmington Downs. The prayers of the monks, who saw it coming, caused the rock to fall short, thereby creating the outlier. Although it has been the setting for many strange occurrences, including the intermittent appearance of a ghostly black dog (which is thought to be a harbinger of death), Meon Hill is most famous for being the scene of an unsolved murder that took place on St Valentine's Day, 14 February 1945. At the time, more than 1,000 prisoners of war were being held in the nearby RAF camp at Long Marston. The body of the elderly victim, Charles Walton of Lower Quinton, was found lying face up, his neck impaled by the tines of a pitchfork. The gashes on his chest and head suggested that a ritual sacrifice had taken place. Indeed, local gossip talked of witchcraft, especially after research discovered that a similar killing had taken place in 1875 at Long Compton, not too many miles away.

Mickleton and Meon Hill, from Dover's Hill

Meon Hill, from Ilmington Downs

Lying at the foot of the north-west escarpment, less than two miles north-east of Broadway, is the Gloucestershire village of Willersey. It is noted for its long spacious green, flanked on either side by stone-built houses and cottages dating from the mid-seventeenth century. Some of the barns have now been converted into houses. Opposite the gabled Bell Inn, and overlooking the village duck pond, stands the late-seventeenth-century Pool House, with its distinctive stone gate pillars. Before the Dissolution, the abbots of Evesham Abbey owned the manor and maintained a summer residence in the village. The cruciform church of St Peter, dating from Norman times, boasts a thirteenth-century north porch and a fifteenth-century tower, with pinnacles and gargoyles. On Willersey Hill, above the village, are the earthwork remains of an Iron Age hillfort.

Willersey

Dover's Hill

At Dover's Hill, above the market town of Chipping Campden, the Cotswold escarpment forms a natural amphitheatre, with extensive views across the Vale of Evesham to Stratford-upon-Avon, Birmingham, the Malvern Hills and the Black Mountains of Wales. The hill is named after Robert Dover, a Norfolk attorney who settled in the area in 1611. Soon after, he founded the Cotswold 'Olympick' Games, held annually on the hill (except during the Civil War) until 1851, when increased rowdiness, caused by invading gangs of hooligans from the industrial towns of the Midlands, led to its abandonment the following year. Although revived in 1951, the games did not include the more popular events such as shin-kicking, in which contestants, wearing metal-tipped boots and holding shoulders or hands, tried to kick each other. Today the games are held on the first Friday after Whitsun, followed the next day by the Scuttlebrook Wake – originally a pagan festival held to celebrate the coming of spring.

Nestling in a hollow at the north-western edge of the Cotswold Hills lies the ancient market town of Chipping Campden, which is dominated by the elegant Perpendicular tower of the church of St James. This building, which replaced an earlier Norman church, dates from the thirteenth century, when Campden began to flourish as an important centre for the export of wool. It was around this time, incidentally, that the town gained the prefix 'Chipping', meaning 'market place'. Campden's prosperity reached its peak in the latter half of the fifteenth century. This wealth is reflected not only in its glorious 'wool' church, but also in many of the houses that line the long, curving High Street. Grevel House, for example, was built in 1380 by William Grevel, who was financier to Richard II and, according to a brass in the church, 'the flower of the wool merchants of all England'.

The Market Hall, Chipping Campden

The Parish Church of St James,
Chipping Campden

Another benefactor to both the town and church was Sir Baptist Hicks, created 1st Viscount Campden in 1628, who erected a magnificent mansion on land adjacent to the church in 1613. Burned down during the Civil War, all that essentially survives today are the lodges and gateway. Hicks also built the celebrated row of almshouses, which lead to the church, and the equally famous Market Hall of 1627 (now owned by the National Trust). In 1902, the early-eighteenth-century Silk Mill, situated in Sheep Street, became the main workshops of the Guild of Handicraft, founded in London by C R Ashbee, who was a major figure of the Arts and Crafts Movement. Although the Guild went into voluntary liquidation in 1907, several distinguished designers and craftsmen – including the descendants of the silversmith George Hart – still operate workshops in the town.

Little is known about the early history of Broad Campden, a small hamlet lying less than a mile south-east of Chipping Campden. Apparently, its earliest recorded mention is in a document dating from 1216, when it was called Parva (Little) Campden. The later change of prefix to 'Broad' may refer to the fact that the houses of the former farming settlement were widely spread across the hillside. The Norman chapel, converted into a house by C R Ashbee in the early twentieth century, dates from the eleventh or twelfth century. Before the Dissolution it was owned by Tewkesbury Abbey. The church of St Michael is Victorian, while the Quaker Meeting House dates from 1663. In the first half of the eighteenth century, a farmer named Jonathan Hull (or Hulls), from Broad Campden, designed and built an experimental steamboat. Its failure caused the locals to compose this doggerel: 'Jonathan Hull, / With his paper skull, [mechanic's cap] / Tried to make a machine / To go against wind and steam. / But he, like an ass, / Couldn't bring it to pass / So at last was ashamed to be seen.'

Main Street, Broad Campden

During Medieval times, the hamlet of Westington, which adjoins Chipping Campden, was – like neighbouring Broad Campden – mainly occupied by farmers and agricultural workers. At that time, the surrounding land consisted of large, open, arable fields and tracts of uncultivated common land (it was not enclosed by drystone walls or hedges until the eighteenth century onwards). Most of the houses in both hamlet and town are built of mellow-golden oolitic limestone from the quarry on Westington Hill. These include Shepherd's Close, Westington Manor and the little ogee-roofed conduit house beside the road, above Westington. The latter was built by Sir Baptist Hicks to supply spring water to the row of almshouses, near Campden's parish church (and later to his Jacobean mansion). 'Pike Cottage', at the southern end of Sheep Street, is so named because it was once the home of the keeper of one of several turnpike toll-gates built around Chipping Campden in the early nineteenth century. At the crossroads at the top of the road leading from 'Pike Cottage', past Westington and up Westington Hill is an unusual signpost bearing an image of four hands, each with a pointing finger. Erected in 1699, the post indicates that distances to Oxford, Worcester, Gloucester and Warwick are several miles shorter than they in fact are. Tradition says that the heads of executed sheep-stealers and thieves were impaled on an iron spike on top of the post.

'Shepherd's Close',
Westington

'Pike Cottage',
Westington

From the honeypot village of Broadway, the road (now blocked by a bypass opened in 1998) climbed steeply up the sheep-grazed escarpment of Fish Hill to the summit of Broadway or Beacon Hill – at 1,024 feet above sea-level, the second highest point in the Cotswolds. Broadway Tower, a folly designed at the late eighteenth century by James Wyatt for the 6th Earl of Coventry, now stands in the grounds of a country park. Among the exhibits inside the building is a display on William Morris,

Broadway Tower,
Broadway Hill

who stayed in the tower many times, together with the Victorian painter Edward Burne-Jones and the Pre-Raphaelite artist Dante Gabriel Rossetti. Broadway Hill is also the site of a notorious execution, in which three people – a mother and her two sons – were hanged for a murder they could not have committed – for, in 1663, two years after their deaths, the alleged murder victim turned up in Chipping Campden, relating an incredible story of kidnapping, slavery in Turkey and eventual escape. The mystery, known as 'The Campden Wonder', has never been adequately resolved.

Cotswold escarpment,
from Fish Hill

At the foot of the Cotswold escarpment, below Broadway Tower, lies the world-famous village of Broadway, with its long, wide main street, two churches and attractive honey-coloured stone houses and cottages, which date mainly from the sixteenth and seventeenth centuries. The village's oldest church, dedicated to St Eadburgha, dates from about 1200, but it has been considerably altered and enlarged over the subsequent centuries. The Millennium Stone, inside, commemorates the passing of 1,000 years since King Edgar granted Broadway to the Benedictine monastery at Pershore in 972. In 1840, increasing development of the village around the present High Street, about a mile from St Eadburgha's, led to the building of a new and nearer church, St Michael and All Angels. The

Old School and Tudor House, Broadway

Broadway, from Burhill

St Eadburgha's Church, Broadway

Lygon Arms, formerly the White Hart, is undoubtedly the most famous of all the inns and hotels to be found in the village (once an important staging-post on the coach road between Worcester and London). The building, dating from the sixteenth century, takes its name from General Edward Lygon (1785–1863), one of Wellington's commanders at Waterloo, who once owned the property. Its present appearance is mainly due to Sydney Russell, who bought the dilapidated hotel in 1904 and restored it to its former glory. His son, Sir Gordon Russell (1892–1980), the noted furniture-maker and furniture designer, opened showrooms in both Broadway and London. The three-gabled Tudor House, found higher up the High Street, dates from the seventeenth century, while the eighteenth-century building next door was originally an inn. It was a school from Victorian times until World War I. The clock was erected in 1887 to commemorate Queen Victoria's Golden Jubilee.

From Broadway, the Cotswold Way heads south-west, climbs over the brow of Burhill and follows the Cotswold escarpment – above Buckland, Laverton and Stanton – to Shenberrow Hill. On the summit of Shenberrow Hill are the earthwork remains of an Iron Age and later Romano-British settlement. The hill may also have been occupied much earlier, as a nearby group of Bronze Age barrows (south-west of Snowshill) was found to contain the 3,000-year-old bones of a warrior, together with a stone battle-axe, a large bronze dagger and a bronze spearhead. Several ancient roads and tracks can be traced in the locality. The White Way, which is closest to the burial sites, runs from Gloucester to Chipping Campden, Stratford-upon-Avon and beyond. The earthwork remains of a prehistoric fort can also be found on the top of Burhill, above Buckland.

Cotswold ridge, near

Shenberrow Hill

*Manor cottages,
Snowshill*

Snowshill Manor

Sited at the head of a deep coomb, below Oat Hill, is the upland village of Snowshill. Its manor, barns and cottages all cluster around a triangular drystone-walled green containing the parish church. During Anglo-Saxon times the estate was granted to Winchcombe Abbey, whose property it remained until the Dissolution. The Victorian church of St Barnabas stands on the site of an earlier foundation, possibly dedicated to St George. Snowshill Manor (now owned by the National Trust) dates from about 1500, but it was considerably altered and enlarged in the seventeenth and eighteenth centuries. Today it houses a unique collection of strange and unusual objects, ranging from toys, musical instruments and clocks to Japanese armour, Tibetan scrolls and Persian lamps. These curios, jam-packed into every corner, were collected by the human magpie Charles Paget Wade, who purchased the property in 1919. Each room in the house was given a name: 'Seventh Heaven', for example, contains many of Wade's childhood toys, while the attic of the south front is known as 'The Room of a Hundred Wheels'. Despite being wealthy, Wade lived – without electricity and central heating – in a small cottage next to the Manor. In monastic times the cottage was a priest's house, and later it was used as a brewhouse. The terraced garden has been attractively laid out as a series of interconnected outdoor 'rooms', some containing pools.

Snowshill, from Shenberrow Hill

Nestling in a secluded hollow at the foot of Burhill (part of the north-west Cotswold escarpment), the manor of Buckland belonged to the monastery of St Peter at Gloucester from Anglo-Saxon times until the Dissolution. The stone-built 'Old Rectory' has an impressive timber-roofed hall dating from the fifteenth century. According to David Verey it is, 'the oldest and most complete medieval parsonage house in the county still so used'. Before going to America in 1735, John Wesley was a frequent visitor to the 'Old Rectory' and often preached in the medieval

The 'Old Rectory',
Buckland

'Brookside', Buckland

church of St Michael. The fifteenth-century glass in the east window of the church is reputed to have come from Hailes Abbey at the Dissolution. It so impressed William Morris that he paid to have it releaded himself. Other treasures inside the church include the fifteenth-century 'Buckland Cope' (a blue-velvet vestment embroidered with pomegranates) and the sixteenth-century 'Mazer' (a maple-wood bowl, painted green on the outside and white inside, and bearing the silver-gilt impression of a saint slaying a dragon).

Stanton

Parish church, Stanton

Set against the wooded backdrop of the steep Cotswold escarpment, Stanton is an attractive golden-stone village with a medieval church, manor house and cross. Most of the houses and cottages – built in traditional Cotswold style – date from the early seventeenth century. Their present well-preserved condition is largely due to the wealthy Lancashire architect and engineer Philip Stott (later Sir Philip), who acquired the estate in 1906 and, over the next thirty years, devoted much time and money to restoring the village and installing a water supply. The church of St Michael and All Angels contains two pulpits: one dating from *c.*1375 and the other from 1684. At the back of the nave the carved ends of the medieval pews have been gouged deep by the chains of shepherds' dogs. Among the monuments in the church are those of the Warrens, who owned the medieval manor house (Warren House), and the Izod and Wynniatt families, who lived in the Jacobean mansion, Stanton Court. A seventeenth-century sundial and globe top the medieval shaft and base of the village cross.

Although the roads to Buckland, Laverton and Stanton lead only to each particular village and nowhere else, the road to Stanway, from the low-lying Vale of Evesham, climbs steeply to the top of the Cotswold escarpment, before heading east to Stow-on-the-Wold and beyond. Situated at the foot of the ancient Stane (or Stone) Way, Stanway House – owned by the Earls of Wemyss and currently the home of Lord Neidpath – was built in Elizabethan and Jacobean times using golden limestone from nearby Coscombe Quarry. The gatehouse is probably the work of Timothy Strong, who was the master-mason of Little Barrington. Above the entrance are the arms of the

Gatehouse and church, Stanway

Tracy family, who acquired the manor from Tewkesbury Abbey after the Dissolution. Within the landscaped grounds is a timber-framed tithe barn, built for the Abbot of Tewkesbury in the fourteenth century. The nearby church of St Peter dates from the twelfth century, but was heavily restored in Victorian times. The village's war memorial sports a fine bronze of St George and the Dragon by Alexander Fisher, a stone column and plinth by Sir Philip Stott and lettering by Eric Gill.

Cutsdean Farm and church, Cutsdean

High on the wolds, above Stanway and the Cotswold escarpment, the farming hamlet of Cutsdean was anciently an outlier of Worcestershire, until boundary changes in 1931 placed it in Gloucestershire. It lies on the slopes of the valley of the infant Windrush, in an area of wold country that is sparsely populated, with isolated farmsteads, few roads and even fewer settlements. In addition to the medieval church of St James, which was rebuilt in Victorian times, the hamlet possesses a restored stone sheepwash, used to wash the sheep prior to shearing. Before the end of the seventh century, the upland country around Cutsdean – stretching eastward towards Blockley and Stow-on-the-Wold – apparently belonged to an Anglo-Saxon called Cod (making it the original Cotswolds). The Windrush, the longest of the truly Cotswold rivers, rises at Field Barn, Taddington, about a mile north of Cutsdean and joins the Thames at Newbridge, seven miles south-west of Oxford.

Once the seat of the Saxon kings of Mercia and the capital of a separate shire, Winchcombeshire, the ancient town of Winchcombe contains a mixture of stone and timber-framed buildings, many of which have mansard roofs (with four sloping sides). The Perpendicular 'wool' church of St Peter, with its exterior gargoyles ('grotesques'), battlements and pinnacles, was built for the parishioners in the mid-fifteenth century, with alterations and additions over subsequent centuries, culminating in the general restoration in the Victorian period. Nothing remains of the great abbey of Winchcombe, originally founded at the close of the eighth century by King Kenelf (or Cenwulf) and dedicated to his martyred son, St Kenelm. According to tradition, the young prince was murdered and his body hidden in a thicket. Miraculously, a dove from heaven carried a note to the Pope in Rome, giving an exact account of the boy's death and the whereabouts of his body. The pilgrims who flocked to the saint's shrine brought great wealth to the abbey, as did its large estates and dealings in wool. After the Dissolution, much of its stone went into the building of the town and nearby Sudeley Castle. The Victorian almshouses of Dent's Terrace were designed by Sir George Gilbert Scott incorporating different coloured stones (not something that Cotswold purists endorse). The Chandos Almshouses were erected in 1573 and rebuilt in 1841.

Winchcombe, from Belas Knap

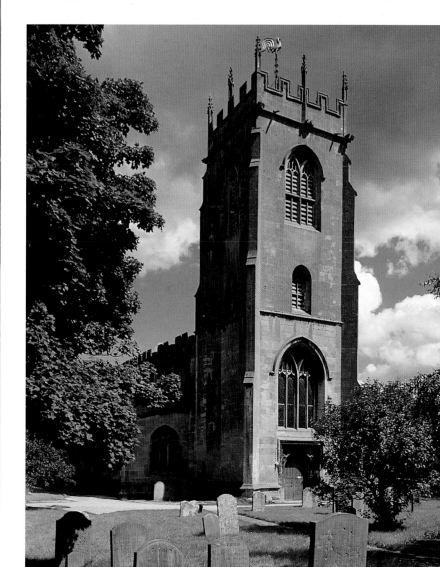

Dent Almshouses,
Winchcombe

Parish church,
Winchcombe

81

Just outside Winchcombe, Sudeley Castle nestles in the 'fat' valley – the name given to the area by the Romans, because it was from here that they received rich tributes of corn and wool. Originally founded in Norman times, the castle was rebuilt in the fifteenth century by the Lancastrian Lord Admiral Ralph Boteler, who succeeded to the estate in 1398. During the Wars of the Roses it was forfeited to the Yorkist Crown, and stayed royal property until Edward IV granted it to his brother, Richard, Duke of Gloucester. Although the castle reverted back to the Crown in 1478, Richard regained ownership when he became King Richard III in 1483. After Henry VIII's death in 1547, his son, Edward VI, granted Sudeley to Sir Thomas Seymour (brother of Jane Seymour, the dead king's third wife). Soon after, Sir Thomas married Henry's

Tithe Barn Garden, Sudeley Castle

widow and sixth and last wife, Catherine Parr. She died in childbirth the following year and was buried in the chapel at Sudeley. Sir Thomas was eventually tried and executed for treason. In 1554, Queen Mary granted the estate to Sir John Brydges, who was created Lord Chandos of Sudeley, and it remained in the family until the early nineteenth century. During the Civil War the castle was badly damaged and the chapel desecrated. Its Victorian restoration and rebuilding were undertaken by Sir George Gilbert Scott and John Drayton Wyatt, while the restorations of the 1930s were carried out by Walter H Godfrey. Nevertheless, Boteler's Banqueting Hall, the Dungeon and the Tithe Barn remain as ruins. Sudeley, now the home of the Dent-Brocklehurst family, is regularly open to the public.

Terrace above Queen's Garden, Sudeley Castle

At 1,083 feet above sea-level – far above the Regency spa town of Cheltenham – the summit of Cleeve Hill is the highest point in the Cotswolds, offering extensive views over the Severn Valley towards the Malvern Hills, the Forest of Dean and the Black Mountains of Wales. The limestone bluff known as Cleeve Cloud reaches 1,040 feet. Both the Hill and Cloud form part of the recreational area and Site of Special Scientific Interest (SSSI) Cleeve Common – the largest of the unenclosed Cotswold commons, covering an area of more than 1,330 acres, much of it grazed by sheep. It also contains the scars of limestone quarrying and a golf course. The word 'Cleeve' is derived from the Old English for 'cliff'. The limestone of the escarpment and plateau hereabouts – being the lowest and oldest stratum of the rock – is known as Inferior Oolite (towards Oxford it is found under the younger Great Oolite). Among the prehistoric earthworks at Cleeve are an Iron Age hillfort and a wide circular enclosure, known as The Ring. More earthworks can be found on the great promontory of Nottingham Hill, to the north. From its source on the windswept Common, the River Isbourne flows northward past Winchcombe to Evesham, where it joins the Warwickshire Avon. Cleeve Hill, Cloud and Common are traversed by the 100-mile Cotswold Way, stretching from Chipping Campden in the north to Bath in the south.

Cleeve Hill and Nottingham Hill

Built of stone and covered with earth, the long barrow or chambered tomb of Belas Knap – on the hill above Humblebee Wood, two miles south of Winchcombe – dates from Neolithic times, 5,000 years ago. Surrounded by a drystone wall, it measures about twelve feet in height, 180 feet in length and sixty feet in width at the northern end. After being ruined by numerous excavations, notably those during Victorian times, the monument was carefully restored in the late 1920s. The entrance passages to the various chambers – including the false portal at the northern end (built to distract grave robbers or, possibly, evil

spirits) – were originally sealed but are now open. Much of the original prehistoric drystone walling survives, proving that the craft has remained unchanged for thousands of years. The remains of over thirty people were unearthed in the tomb, including (in the rubble behind the false portal) the skull of a man and the bones of five children. The name 'Belas Knap' is thought by some to derive from the Old English for a 'beacon on a hillock'. Others claim that 'Belas' is a personal name, or the name of a god.

Belas Knap long barrow

Humblebee How, near Belas Knap

Despite more recent claims that the name 'Cotswolds' is derived from 'Cod's Weald', or the 'high open ground of an Anglo-Saxon landowner called Cod', the sixteenth-century antiquarian William Camden, along with many others, considered that the origin of the word came from 'cotes' (sheep folds) and 'wolds' (open, uncultivated hills). Indeed, the latter seems far more appropriate, given that the wolds have supported sheep since prehistoric times, and wool from the animals' backs has provided the wealth to create almost all of the magnificent houses, mansions and churches so characteristic of the region. During the Middle Ages vast flocks of sheep, known as 'Cotswold Lions' – introduced into Britain by the Romans – were bred for their long wool, which was initially exported raw to Europe, and later manufactured into cloth. The Cotswold wool and cloth industry grew and prospered to such an extent that it dominated the country's economy for several centuries. Medieval Flemish weavers produced such excellent cloth from the raw fleeces that they asserted: 'In Europe the best wool is English, in England the best wool is Cotswold.' The 'golden fleece' brought great wealth to the wool and cloth merchants, many of whom had themselves immortalized in the brass, glass and stone of the 'wool' churches they endowed. The eventual decline of the wool and cloth industry, together with the consumer trend towards a small joint of meat with a minimum of fat, brought the Cotswold Lion sheep breed close to the brink of extinction. Today, because of the efforts of some dedicated individuals, encouraged by organizations such as the Cotswold Sheep Society and the Rare Breeds Survival Trust, this large-boned, heavy-fleeced animal is flourishing once more. Its distinctive feature is a forelock of fine wool, traditionally left on at shearing. Many of the sheep now grazing the wolds are mongrels, one of the most popular being the 'mule', which has been cross-bred from a Bluefaced Leicester ram and a hardy Scottish Blackface ewe. Another, the Colbred, was created by a Cotswold farmer in the 1950s.

Cotswold Lion

The 'Fat' Valley, near Winchcombe

The villages of Temple Guiting (Upper Guiting) and Guiting Power (Lower Guiting) lie in the valley of the River Windrush, roughly midway between Winchcombe and Bourton-on-the-Water. 'Guiting' is derived from the Old English *gyte*, meaning 'gush' or 'flood'. Temple Guiting takes the first part of its name from the fact that the manor belonged to the Knights Templar in the twelfth century. 'Power' comes from the Le Poer family, who held lands at Lower Guiting in the thirteenth and fourteenth centuries. The dwellings of Guiting Power cluster around the Square, with its triangular village green and memorial cross of medieval design. In addition to commemorating the dead of World War I, the cross stands as a reminder of the attempt to establish a market in the village in the early fourteenth century. The church of St Michael, with its Perpendicular tower, stands at the southern end of the village. Dating from Norman times, it was rescued from decay in the early twentieth century.

Strung out for almost a mile along the narrow valley of the infant Windrush, the upland village of Naunton spreads eastward from the church of St Andrew towards the former corn mill (now a private residence) – with the stream running along the backs of the stone-built houses and cottages (rather than in front like those to be found at Bourton-on-the-Water). Local tradition says that the village was founded by an imp who fell out of the sky while flying over the wolds with 'Satan and his angels'. Unable to follow his master because of a broken wing, the imp built the first dwelling, which eventually developed into the linear settlement seen today. Indeed, according to E F Eales, the rector of Naunton from 1902 to 1926, 'In the character of the people of these hills there is often a strain of impishness to be found. Many of Dickens's quaint characters are here still in the flesh; some of them most delightful characters, others exasperatingly impossible ones.' Among the buildings of interest in Naunton according to Eales is a four-gabled dovecote 'containing 1,175 pigeon nests'.

Naunton

91

The villages of Upper and Lower Slaughter – both watered by the little River Eye, a tributary of the Dikler and Windrush – lie within a mile of each other, north of Bourton-on-the-Water. Several explanations for the name 'Slaughter' have been suggested, none referring to a scene of bloodshed. Some say that it is derived from the Old English *slohtre* meaning 'slough' or 'muddy place', while others maintain that it refers to the abundance of sloe trees, or blackthorns, in the locality.

The Eye (known as the Slaughter Brook in the stretch between the two villages) rises in the wolds above Eyford Park, where, according to Samuel Rudder, the 'inimitable' John Milton (1608–74) wrote part of his epic poem *Paradise Lost*. Upper Slaughter stands on a hillside above the brook, which is crossed by several stone footbridges and a ford. F E Witts, a former lord of the manor who was also rector of St Peter's church from 1808 until his death in 1854, wrote *The Diary of a Cotswold Parson*. The brick-built corn mill at Lower Slaughter, with its tall chimney and working waterwheel, dates from the nineteenth century. It is now a museum and shop with craft displays. The church of St Mary and the seventeenth-century manor house, with its large, sixteenth-century dovecote, stand at the opposite end of the village. Most of the stone cottages, which overlook the shallow trout-filled brook, date from the late sixteenth or early seventeenth century.

Mill and cottages, Lower Slaughter

Brook and cottages, Lower Slaughter

Spanned by low stone bridges, the fast-flowing River Windrush runs alongside the tree-dappled green at Bourton-on-the-Water to create such a delightful scene that the village has often been called 'the Venice of the Cotswolds'. At the end of the eighteenth century, Rudder wrote: 'Many of the houses are ranged into a street, tho' somewhat irregularly, on each side of this natural canal, the banks of which being well gravelled, and rarely over-flow'd, afford a delightful walk.' The original settlement grew up on the south-western edge of the Salmonsbury Iron Age camp (also used by the Romans) and just east of the point where the Roman Fosse Way and Buckle Street (or Ryknild Street) cross the Windrush. The Norman church of St Lawrence, built on Anglo-Saxon foundations, was largely demolished in 1784 and then rebuilt in neo-classical style with a tower topped by a lead-covered dome. In Victorian times the church was again rebuilt,

while retaining the Georgian tower and the fourteenth-century chancel. Situated behind the Old New Inn is a one-ninth scale model of the village, constructed in the late 1930s. Within this is another model village – complete with yet another. The oldest of the stone bridges at Bourton was built in 1754. It stands in front of the 'Old Corn Mill', which is now the home of the Cotswolds Motor Museum and Village Life Exhibition. The newest is the Coronation Bridge, erected in 1953. Before the erection of the bridges, the river was crossed by a series of fords. Downstream from Bourton, the Windrush is joined by the combined waters of the Eye and Dikler.

'The Old Corn Mill', Bourton-on-the-Water

Bourton-on-the-Water

The three Rissington villages – Wyck, Little and Great – all lie along the sheltered slopes of a windswept ridge, east of the Dikler and Windrush valleys. The village of Wyck Rissington, the most northerly of the trio, is grouped around two centres – one being the church and the other a large green with a pond. Most of the cottages were built in the seventeenth and eighteenth centuries. The church of St Laurence, which is Norman in origin, was largely rebuilt in the thirteenth century. In the south wall of the chancel of the church is a stained glass lancet window depicting the Crucifixion. Dating from the fourteenth century, it is unusual in that the cross is coloured green. Although the sun appears to be red, there is a theory that it is shown in eclipse and it is, therefore, the moon in front that is red. However, a crescent moon, tinted blue, can be clearly seen on the opposite side of the cross. The mosaic, elsewhere in the church, serves as a reminder that a maze once existed in the village. It was created by the rector, Canon Harry Cheales, and destroyed after his death in 1984.

Village pump, Wyck Rissington

Midway between Burford and Witney, the Oxfordshire village of Minster Lovell lies mostly on the southern bank of the Windrush, with, essentially, an inn, a street of cottages (including 'The Old Post House'), the parish church and the ruins of a manor house on the north. The village takes its name from the medieval church or 'minster' (served by a tiny alien priory) and from the Lovell family, who were lords of the manor from at least the twelfth century. In 1414, the priory, belonging to the Benedictine abbey of Ivry in Normandy, was dissolved and its lands seized by the Crown. The minster and the Lovell's old manor house were demolished by William, 7th Baron Lovell of Tichmarsh, some twenty or so years later. The former, dedicated to St John, was replaced with the present cruciform church, dedicated to St Kenelm, and the latter with Minster Lovell Hall (now a ruin in the care of English Heritage). The last of the Lovells, Francis, the 9th baron, was declared a traitor and his lands confiscated after fighting on the losing side at the battle of Bosworth Field in 1485. Although he was allegedly killed at the battle of Stoke, near Newark, in 1487, tradition says that he returned to Minster Lovell and was secretly locked in an underground room by one of the servants. Tragically,

TOP *Parish church and Minster Lovell Hall*

ABOVE *'The Old Post House', Minster Lovell*

the servant suddenly died, causing Lovell himself to perish from starvation. Apparently, a seated skeleton (presumed to be the remains of the fugitive) was discovered in a large underground vault at Minster Lovell in 1708.

The bustling Oxfordshire town of Burford is centred along a wide north-south High Street, which drops steeply from a major crossroads high on the wolds to end at an old stone bridge spanning the River Windrush. Despite being a major market town – still preserving its medieval layout – Burford has no central market square. Trading was carried out in the main street and side alleys, while tolls were collected in the twin-gabled 'Tolsey' or market hall (now a museum). During the Middle Ages the main road ran east-west through the centre of the town

and past the Tolsey. This route eventually declined in importance – notably in the early nineteenth century, when the track along the top of the hill to the south was made into a turnpike road. As a result, through traffic, especially horse-drawn coaches, found it no longer necessary to descend the steep street into the town, and trade sharply declined. A new coaching inn was subsequently built at the top of the hill. The houses in Burford – the earliest dating from at least the fourteenth century – make attractive use of local natural materials: stone from nearby quarries and timber from the once extensive Forest of Wychwood. The 'wool' church of St John the Baptist, located in the oldest part of the town, near an ancient ford across the river, dates from Norman times (incorporating fragments of an earlier foundation). The church has undergone alterations and additions over subsequent centuries, culminating in the fifteenth-century remodelling, which included the construction of an elegant spire and grand porch. William Morris was so upset when he saw G E Street's Victorian restoration of the building that, on his arrival at Broadway Tower in 1876, he drafted the letter to *The Athenaeum* that led to the formation of the Society for the Protection of Ancient Buildings. The almshouses near the church were founded in 1457.

High Street, Burford

Almshouses and church,
Burford

Strung out along the valley of the Sherborne Brook, a tributary of the Windrush, Sherborne was a divided medieval village, with 'Eastende' separated from 'West-ende' by the manor belonging to Winchcombe Abbey. Today Sherborne Park Estate belongs to the National Trust, as does the seventeenth-century 'Lodge Park', which was originally built not as a dwelling house but as a vantage point from which to view the coursing of deer

by greyhounds. Sherborne House, dating from the latter half of the sixteenth century and rebuilt in the nineteenth century, has now been converted into luxury apartments. Most of the houses at the western end of the village, known locally as 'Top End', date from the seventeenth to nineteenth centuries; while most of those at the eastern end, or 'Bottom End' (including the cottages in the photograph above), were rebuilt in the nineteenth century as part of a model village.

Estate Cottages,
Sherborne

Broadwater Bottom,
near Turkdean

In the high wolds of the north-west Cotswolds, the limestone has been weathered to a smooth surface, with gentle undulations cut by river valleys. The light soil, although poor, manages to support grass, crops, flowers and pockets of trees. In the area around Turkdean, north of Northleach, much of the pasture has been transformed into arable land, the main crops being wheat, barley and oats. Near a spring, in a field north of Turkdean, a three-day excavation carried out in 1998 conducted by the Channel 4 television programme *Time Team*, revealed the site of an extensive Romano-British villa. Among the artefacts unearthed were oyster shells (possibly from the north Kent coast), a child's bracelet, coins, an enamelled brooch with the Latin message 'Be Happy', and the metal remains of a large wooden chest. After the programme had been completed, in order to deter treasure-seekers and 'rogue metal detectorists', the site was seeded with pennies to the value of £500.

Sited at an important crossroads, just off the Fosse Way, Northleach was at one time a great market town, celebrated throughout Europe as a major centre of the Cotswold wool trade. The fifteenth-century church of St Peter and St Paul, paid for out of the pockets of the wealthy wool merchants, is reputed to have been built with stone dug from a quarry in the town itself, more precisely in what is now the Market Square. Indeed, evidence of quarrying in the form of subterranean tunnels has been confirmed over the years, notably in 1937, when the ground collapsed near 'The Guggle' cottage (opposite the fire station), revealing a sixty-feet-deep hole with shafts radiating out from the centre. One such tunnel is said to lead to the church. In addition to being embellished with beautifully carved stonework, the church contains many fine memorial brasses depicting its benefactors, some of whom are shown standing on the woolsacks and sheep that made them so rich.

Northleach

From the Kilkenny viewpoint, situated a mile or so south-west of Andoversford, the high wolds spread eastwards towards Bourton-on-the-Water, with tightly packed villages such as Notgrove, Turkdean, Hazleton and the Shiptons nestling in the folds of the undulating hills. The viewpoint is said to derive its name from a nearby farm, originally named 'Kilkenny' after Oliver Cromwell captured the Irish town of Kilkenny in 1650. A prehistoric enclosure is thought to have existed at the viewpoint site, but all evidence of it has now been effectively obliterated by quarrying for limestone. The nearby round barrow or burial mound is known as 'St Paul's Epistle'. One suggestion regarding the origin of its curious name is that it derives from the ancient custom of 'beating the bounds' (marking parish boundaries), during which a few verses from the Bible would be read aloud. The River Churn rises in a small dell at Seven Springs, a few miles west of Kilkenny. It was once argued that the spot was the true source of the River Thames (rather than Thames Head, near Cirencester).

High wolds, from Kilkenny Viewpoint

In *A New History of Gloucestershire* (1779), Rudder lists three Brockhamptons: one in Cleeve, another in Snowshill, and the third in Sevenhampton. Cleeve is a small hamlet, situated below the Cotswold escarpment and on the northern outskirts of Cheltenham. Snowshill, then a settlement consisting of two farms – Great and Little Brockhampton – is now essentially just a single farm. While Sevenhampton, which is located on the high wolds south of Winchcombe, is the largest and most compact of the three settlements. Indeed, it is large enough to be considered a village. On its western side lies Brockhampton Park, with its large Tudor-style mansion, built in the Victorian period and incorporating an earlier house dating from about 1639. Apparently, winters can persist for so long in this area that in 1634 the snow and ice did not clear until August.

Brockhampton Park

On the quarried edge of Leckhampton Hill, overlooking the Georgian spa town of Cheltenham, stands a prominent, freestanding pillar of limestone known as the Devil's Chimney. Legend says that the chimney rises straight from hell, and that the Devil is trapped deep inside the rock below. Out of fear of setting him free or, alternatively, because it was in danger of collapse from erosion, the pillar was strengthened with iron rods and mortar in 1985. Although climbing the rock pinnacle is now strictly prohibited, a record number of thirteen people once stood together on its top. The limestone that was used for the building of Georgian Cheltenham came from the quarries on Leckhampton Hill. From 1798, it was transported in trucks from the hilltop, down the edge of the scarp and into the vale, by a primitive gravity-powered inclined railway.

The Devil's Chimney,

Leckhampton Hill

From Crickley Hill, approximately four miles south of Cheltenham, the Cotswold escarpment sweeps south-west in an arc – past Barrow Wake, The Peak and Birdlip Hill – to Cooper's Hill (the site of an annual cheese-rolling competition, in which contestants chase cheeses down the steep slope at breakneck speed). At around 900 feet above sea-level, the views from the Barrow Wake vantage point – over the Vale of Gloucester to the River Severn, the Malverns and to Wales beyond – are spectacular. In the photograph, the distant, rounded limestone outlier on the right is Robin's Wood Hill (beyond the city of Gloucester); the tree-topped Cooper's Hill is in the middle; with the wooded Cotswold escarpment around The Peak and Birdlip Hill on the left. It was in an Iron Age burial mound at Barrow Wake that the finely worked Birdlip mirror and other treasures were discovered. These are now preserved in Gloucester City Museum.

Cotswold escarpment,
from Barrow Wake

An old market town of silver-grey stone buildings, Painswick – 'the Queen of the Cotswolds' – was a thriving centre of the cloth industry from the arrival of a colony of Flemish weavers in the sixteenth century until production declined in the nineteenth century. Reflecting the former prosperity of the hill town are many fine houses and mansions, including the seventeenth-century Castle Hale; the gabled Court House, dating from *c.*1604; Dover House from *c.*1720; and the eighteenth-century Painswick House, set in parkland on the northern outskirts. The ancient stone and half-timbered post office in New Street is constructed around a cruck frame; while the Little Fleece, formerly part of an inn and now let as a

Painswick Hill, from Painswick Beacon

bookshop, is owned by the National Trust. The soaring steeple of the parish church of St Mary was struck by a bolt of lightning in 1883, bringing a thirty-feet section of it crashing down into the nave. Many of the churchyard's magnificent table tombs (probably the work of the local Bryan family of stonemasons) are late seventeenth and eighteenth century. The ninety-nine clipped yews, for which the churchyard is famous, were planted at the end of the eighteenth century, and are said to be uncountable. Impressive views of the area, including the Severn valley, can be obtained from Painswick Beacon, the summit of which is 930 feet above sea-level.

Parish church, Painswick   *Painswick*

A little more than a mile west of Painswick and three miles north of Stroud, the former cloth-making village of Edge, with its houses, farms and Victorian church, stands at the top of the Cotswold escarpment, overlooking the Vale of Gloucester. On Cud Hill – found some two miles north of the village, beyond Hudinknoll Hill – is a small, square, stone building, with open arches on three sides (the arch on the fourth side has been blocked). Built by Winifred Blow as a memorial to her husband, Detmar Blow (an architect associated with the Arts and Crafts Movement), the structure was never completed because of the outbreak of World War II. The nearby grave of the couple is marked with a stone carved with lettering by the typographer Eric Gill. Their country house, Hilles, was designed by the architect himself and stands further south, near Hudinknoll Hill.

Edge and Hudinknoll Hill, from Scottsquar Hill

Almost 800 feet above sea-level, Bisley stands on an isolated plateau partly encircled by the valley of the Frome (the tributary river of the Severn, which rises near Birdlip and sweeps in an arc south-west to Stroud). The grey-stone village is noted for its ancient springs, the waters of which are reputed to possess special healing properties. It is known that the Romans worshipped at altars here, and even today some 2,000 years later, the wellheads are dressed with flowers on Ascension Day each year. Near the parish church of All Saints, the sacred waters emerge from seven springs, known as Bisley Wells. The structure, set into the hillside, was restored in 1863 by Thomas Keble, vicar of Bisley and younger brother of John Keble (one of the leaders of the Oxford Movement and author of *The Christian Year*, a book of sacred verse published anonymously in 1827). The church stands on a

Parish church, Bisley

Lock-up, Bisley

sacred pre-Christian site, probably associated with the springs. The present building dates from the thirteenth century, but it was restored in Victorian times. In the churchyard is a rare late-thirteenth-century 'Poor Soul's Light', a lantern in which a candle was lit for the deceased souls of the poor. It is said to cover a well in which a former parish priest fell to his death one dark night. Among other buildings of interest in Bisley are the two-celled lock-up, dated 1824; the medieval Over Court, with seventeenth-century alterations; and Wesley House, dating from the sixteenth century.

Strung out along a narrow valley lying north-west of Cirencester, the four Duntisbourne settlements are all named after the Dun Brook. The largest and most northerly, Duntisbourne Abbots (once the property of the abbey of St Peter at Gloucester) is built in terraces down the sides of the valley. The squat, saddleback-towered church of St Peter dates from Norman times, with subsequent alterations and additions, notably in the thirteenth century and during the Victorian period. It stands on high ground in the centre of the village. The road leading south to Duntisbourne Leer becomes the bed of the brook for some thirty yards. It was used to wash the wheels of carts and the hooves of horses, and it is the only surviving water lane found in the Cotswolds. Duntisbourne Leer, its farms and cottages clustered around a shallow ford, belonged to the medieval abbey of Lire in Normandy.

*Parish church,
Duntisbourne Abbots*

*Church and cross,
Duntisbourne Rouse*

The Dun Brook is also crossed by fords located at Middle Duntisbourne and Duntisbourne Rouse. The latter hamlet (named after the Norman Rous family) contains one of the smallest churches in the Cotswolds. It is dedicated to St Michael, and the building boasts herringbone masonry dating from Anglo-Saxon times. Although it was altered during the Norman period and given its tiny saddleback tower in the late sixteenth century (the base is, in fact, earlier), the church is unspoiled by any later restoration work. Having been built on a steep slope above the brook, the building, small as it is, is able to accommodate a vaulted stone crypt beneath the Norman chancel. The carved misericord stalls are believed to have come from Cirencester Abbey after its dissolution. Situated in the churchyard is a fourteenth-century stone cross with a long shaft.

Ford, Duntisbourne Leer

The River Coln, which rises near Andoversford and enters the Thames near Lechlade, lends its name to three settlements along its course – Coln St Dennis, Coln Rogers and Coln St Aldwyns. The most northerly of these is Coln St Dennis, which lies in a small coomb near Fossebridge. This is the point where the Fosse Way spans the river. The latter part of the hamlet's name comes from the abbey of St Dennis in Normandy. Coln Rogers, a mile or so downstream, was once owned by Roger FitzMiles (or Roger of Gloucester), who succeeded to the earldom of Hertford in 1143. Apparently, it was formerly known as Coln St Andrew after the dedication of its church. The largest and most southerly of the three settlements is Coln St Aldwyns, located on the edge of extensive parkland, midway between Bibury and Fairford. Although the church is dedicated to St John the Baptist, it is thought that its original dedication was to St Aldwyn, who was the eighth-century abbot of Partney, Lincolnshire.

St James' Church, Coln St Dennis

Arlington Row, Bibury

Situated below the tree-lined slopes of the Coln valley, about six miles upstream of Fairford, Bibury is a small 'honeypot' village, noted for attracting hoards of visitors, as well as freshwater trout of the most incredible size. The village itself is divided into two parts: Arlington, with its former fulling mill and celebrated row of early-seventeenth-century weaving cottages, on the west side of the river; and Bibury, with its church, school and hotels,

on the east. On the Arlington side, between the Mill Leat and the Coln, is a wildfowl reserve, known as Rack Isle – so called because the wet cloth (having been fulled and dyed) was once hung on racks to dry in the area. Although there was a mill on the Coln at Bibury as far back as Anglo-Saxon times, the present mill (now a museum) dates from the seventeenth century. The neighbouring Trout Farm was founded in 1902 by Arthur Severn.

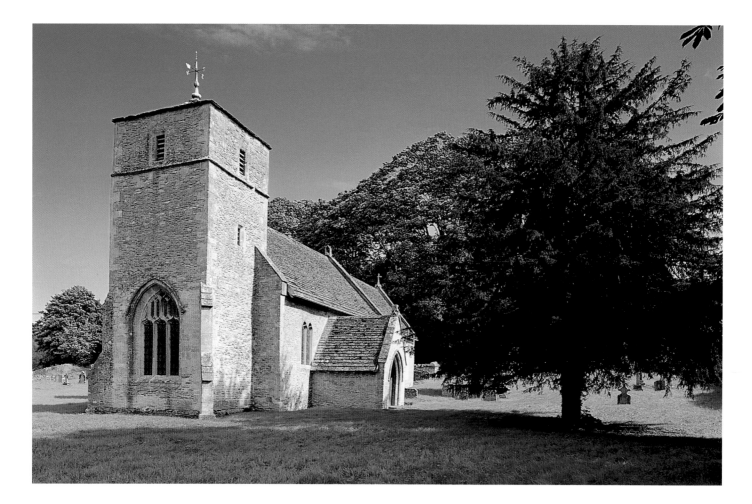

The Gloucestershire villages of Eastleach Martin and Eastleach Turville – situated on opposite sides of the River Leach, some eight miles south-east of Northleach – are connected by an old stone 'clapper' footbridge, known as Keble's Bridge. Reputedly, it was built by John Keble, the celebrated writer of religious verse (*see Bisley, p. 113*), who was rector of both parishes from 1815. The tiny church of St Michael and St Martin at Eastleach Martin (or Bouthrop), on the east bank of the river, dates from the Norman period, but was largely rebuilt in the thirteenth century. The three windows in the fourteenth-century north transept are considered fine examples of the Decorated style. St Andrew's at Eastleach Turville, although Norman in origin, is not quite as old as its neighbour. The saddleback tower is fourteenth century, the north transept thirteenth century, and the richly decorated south doorway mid-twelfth century. Tradition says that the canopied recess behind the organ was the tomb of an abbess, and once contained a beautiful rosary. The carved, medieval lectern is said to have come from Tewkesbury Abbey after the Dissolution. It used to be said that the bells of both churches called to each other across the river: the three bells of St Martin's, claiming 'We-ring-best', and the two of St Andrew's answering 'We too, we too'.

ABOVE **Bouthrop Church, Eastleach Martin**

BELOW **Keble's Bridge, Eastleach Martin**

Just over the Gloucestershire border, a few miles east of Eastleach Martin, is the Oxfordshire village of Filkins (merging to the south-west into the adjacent manor of Broughton Poggs). Although the village has now been by-passed, it originally stood on the main Burford to Swindon road – a great medieval route along which Cotswold wool and cloth was once transported by packhorse and wagon to Southampton for export. Many of the houses in Filkins are fenced with thin slabs, or 'planks', of locally quarried stone. Indeed, the stone – Great Oolite known as Forest Marble – is the most outstanding feature of the village. It is also used for roofs and porches. 'Chapel Cottage', opposite the parish church, derives its name from the Primitive Methodist Chapel, dated 1853, which stands immediately behind the dwelling. As well as containing a small museum and lock-up, Filkins is also the home of the Cotswold Woollen Weavers, who card, spin and weave the wool using traditional methods and machinery.

'Chapel Cottage', Filkins

Poet, designer, craftsman, radical socialist and one of the leaders of the Arts and Crafts Movement, William Morris, leased Kelmscott Manor as a country home from 1871 until his death in 1896. Standing in attractive gardens on the north bank of the upper Thames, some two or three miles downstream from Lechlade, the grey-stone Elizabethan house (with seventeenth-century additions) retains its traditional wooden gutters, mullioned windows and two tall, gabled and slightly tapering north towers. Morris himself wrote of the 'Old House' in 1895: 'The roofs are covered with the beautiful stone slates of the district, the most lovely covering which a roof can have, especially when, as here and in all the traditional old houses of the countryside, they are "sized down"; the smaller ones to the top and the bigger ones towards the eaves, which gives the same sort of pleasure in their orderly

East front, Kelmscott Manor

South front and dove-cote, Kelmscott Manor

beauty as a fish's scales or a bird's feathers.' Kelmscott, however, did not become Morris property until 1913, when his widow, Jane, purchased the manor from its owner and Oxfordshire farmer Robert Hobbs. In 1938, their daughter, May, left the estate in trust to the University of Oxford (the Manor, containing many Morris treasures, is now owned and managed by the Society of Antiquaries of London, and is regularly open to the public). William

Morris lies buried in the churchyard of St George's church at Kelmscott. The Memorial Cottages, near the Manor, were designed by Philip Webb. They sport a stone relief of Morris carved by George Jack. The Manor Cottages next door – built for May Morris in memory of her mother – were designed by Ernest Gimson (1864–1919), as was the village hall (Morris Memorial Hall), completed by Norman Jewson and opened by George Bernard Shaw in 1934.

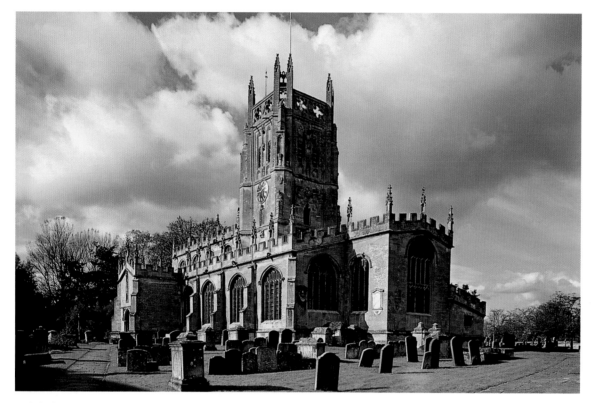

Parish church, Fairford

Originating as a river-crossing settlement on the Coln, the ancient market town of Fairford is dominated by the beautifully proportioned Late Perpendicular 'wool' church of St Mary, with its pinnacled tower, magnificent medieval glass and wealth of carvings, in both stone and wood. The church was rebuilt sometime around the end of the fifteenth century by John Tame, a rich and prosperous wool and cloth merchant. However, the base of the original early-fifteenth-century tower was incorporated into the structure. Rudder wrote that Tame erected the church 'for the sake of placing the glass in it'. Indeed, the stained and painted glass in the windows ranks among the finest in England. To avoid damage they have been removed on several occasions, notably during the Civil War and World War II. Covering an area of more than 2,000 square feet, the twenty-eight windows – known as 'the poor man's Bible' – tried to portray, for the mainly illiterate congregation, a pictorial summary of the Christian faith. Among the subjects covered are the serpent tempting Eve, God appearing to Moses in the burning bush and the birth of Christ and Last Judgement. High up in the nave is a series of small but 'terrible' devils. The deep-gabled millhouse, standing on the banks of the Coln north of the church, dates from the seventeenth century.

Mill and church, Fairford

Shortly after their invasion of Britain in AD 43 the Romans established a frontier fort at a strategic site beside the River Churn, not far from the capital of the British Dobunni tribe at Bagendon. Sited at or near the intersection of three major, formerly military roads – Fosse Way, Ermin Way and Akeman Street – the garrison settlement developed into the administrative centre for the Dobunni, known as Corinium Dobunnorum, and the second largest Roman city in Britain, after London. During Anglo-Saxon times, its name became Coryn Ceastre (Cirencester), meaning the 'fortified town on the Churn'.

Roman remains (apart from those in the Corinium Museum) include an exposed section of the defensive wall in the Abbey Grounds and the grassed-over amphitheatre, south-west of the town. After the Conquest, the Normans erected a great Augustinian abbey in the town, which prospered 'on the backs of Cotswold sheep' until its dissolution in 1539. All that now remains above ground of the monastery is the restored Norman gateway. The town church, dedicated to St John the Baptist and the largest parish church in Gloucestershire, dates from the Norman period, with alterations and additions over subsequent

Parish church,
Cirencester

centuries. The 162-feet-high tower, originally intended to carry a spire, was erected in the fifteenth century. Its unique three-storey south porch, overlooking the market place, was built by the abbey as an administrative centre in *c.*1490. It later served as the town hall, and only became Church property in the eighteenth century. All that survives of St John's Hospital, founded in the twelfth century, is the Norman arcade of the hall. Immediately west of the town, and hidden by a massive yew hedge, stands the eighteenth-century mansion built for the 1st Lord Bathurst, set in the extensive grounds of Cirencester Park.

Town wall in Abbey Grounds, Cirencester

St John's Hospital, Cirencester

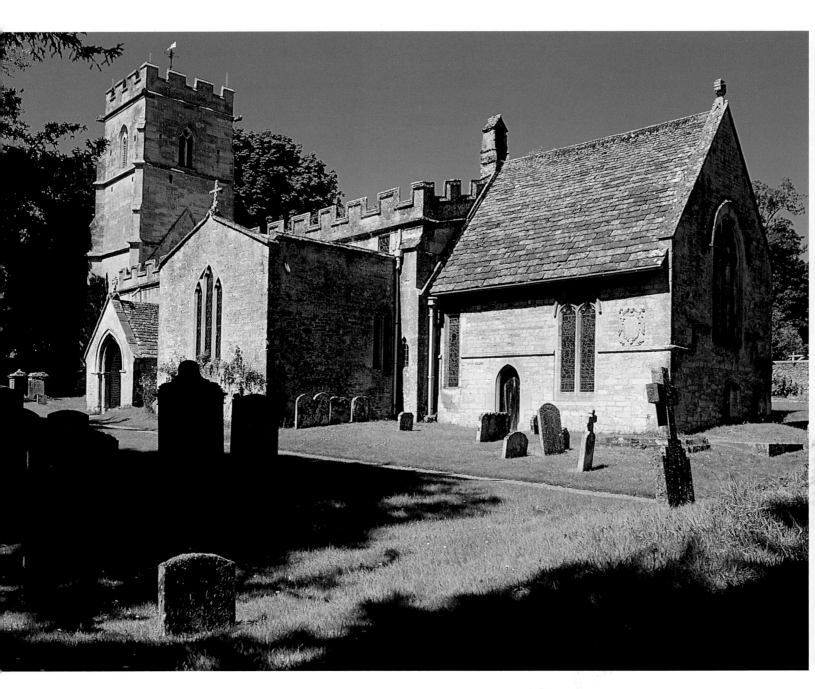

The Ampneys – Ampney Crucis, Ampney St Peter, Ampney St Mary and Down Ampney – are all named after the Ampney Brook, a small tributary of the Thames that rises on the open wolds some four miles north-east of Cirencester. The first three villages stand close to each other on the dipping, pastoral slopes of the hills; the latter – birthplace of the composer Ralph Vaughan Williams (1872–1958) – lies further south, almost in the upper Thames valley. The 'Ivy Church' of Ampney St Mary now stands alone on the banks of the brook because the village was moved to Ashbrook, about a mile north-east. Ampney Crucis, the main nucleus of the three northern villages, is noted for its ancient church, dedicated to the Holy Rood. The north doorway is Anglo-Saxon, the west tower is fifteenth century, the vestry is Victorian and the gable-headed churchyard cross dates from *c*.1410.

Parish church, Ampney Crucis

Minchinhampton

Occupying the tongue of land lying between the 'Golden Valley' of Chalford and the old cloth-making town of Nailsworth, Minchinhampton is a small hilltop market town built of fine-quality, grey stone cut from the nearby quarries. The Market House, standing on stone pillars in the central square, was erected in 1698. This was a time of great prosperity for the wool and cloth merchants of the town, and their wealth is reflected in the many fine seventeenth- and eighteenth-century houses, and the monuments and brasses in the parish church of Holy Trinity. Dating from the Norman period, when, like the town, it belonged to a convent at Caen in Normandy, the church sports a curious truncated spire, which is crowned with a stone coronet (created in 1563 when the top section was in danger of collapse). On Minchinhampton Common (now owned by the National Trust) are the earthwork remains of a massive Iron Age hillfort, known as 'The Bulwarks'.

Some 600 to 700 feet below the bleak, uncultivated pastures of Selsley Common – pockmarked by the remains of prehistoric earthworks – lies the old cloth-making town of Stroud. Its development as the major industrial centre of the Cotswolds was entirely due to its position at the convergence of five 'Golden Valleys', together with its close proximity to the River Severn (to which it was linked by the Stroudwater Canal, opened in 1779). At the height of the town's prosperity there were an estimated 150 mills in the area. Interestingly, some of the houses and bridges are built of Thames valley brick, rather than Cotswold stone. This is because the canal boatmen, taking cloth east to London, found alternative loads for their return journey. Although its prosperity declined in the nineteenth century due to the advent of steam power, Stroud remains a busy industrial and commercial centre, with several factories still producing cloth.

Stroud, from Selsley Common

At the north-eastern edge of the semicircular sweep of Cotswold escarpment overlooking the Cam valley, Frocester Hill offers panoramic views across the Vale of Berkeley to the River Severn, the Forest of Dean and the mountains of Wales beyond. The hill, more than 770 feet high, takes its name from the village of Frocester, down in the vale, four miles south-west of Stroud. Owned by the abbey of Gloucester until the Dissolution, the village is noted for its massive medieval tithe barn, built by Abbot John Gamage in *c.*1300. On the summit of Frocester Hill stands the Nympsfield Neolithic long barrow, its stone-

built chambers, once earth-covered, are now open to the sky. Excavations of the tomb, which is ninety feet long, have unearthed the skeletons of over seventeen individuals, together with pottery, flint tools and a large quantity of pig bones. Examination of the human remains revealed that many suffered from abscesses, rotting teeth and swollen gums. The barrow, almost 5,000 years old, takes its name from the nearby village of Nympsfield, which was once a coaching stop on the road from Bath, down the steep scarp of Frocester Hill, to Gloucester.

Nympsfield long barrow,
Frocester Hill

Vale of Berkeley and River Severn, from Frocester Hill

Hidden in a deep and secluded wooded coomb, or 'bottom', situated less than a mile east of the old cloth-making village of Uley, the stone-built hamlet of Owlpen clusters around a homely Tudor manor house and 'beautified' Victorian church, both with early medieval origins. The manor (regularly open to the public) contains many items of interest, including: the unique painted-cloth wall-hangings in the Great Chamber, which probably date from the late seventeenth century; numerous paintings, drawings and prints associated with the house; and a fascinating collection of Cotswold Arts and Crafts furnishings. Indeed, the Arts and Crafts revival architect Norman Jewson owned the house between 1925 and 1926 and was responsible for its sensitive restoration after many years of gradual decay. Since 1974 the manor has belonged to the Mander family, descendants of the Wolverhampton paint and varnish manufacturer Samuel Theodore Mander, who built Wightwick Manor (now owned by the National Trust, and noted for its Arts and Crafts architecture and furnishings).

Manor and church, Owlpen

In an area lying between Frocester Hill, in the north-east, and Stinchcombe Hill, in the south-west, the Cotswold escarpment forms a natural amphitheatre around the low-lying Cam valley. In the centre of the semicircular valley, much of which is divided into a patch-work of fields, is an almost treeless island hill known as Cam Long Down, at the south-western end of which stands the conical-shaped Peaked Down. According to

legend, the hill was created by the Devil, who, intending to dam the Severn with a gigantic wheelbarrowful of Cotswold stone, was tricked by a cobbler into dumping his load in the valley. On the high escarpment east of Cam Long Down, and above its neighbouring outlier Down-ham Hill, are the earthwork remains of Uleybury hillfort. Covering thirty-two acres, it is one of the largest and most impressive Iron Age promontory forts in the Cotswolds.

Downham Hill and Uleybury, from Peaked Down

Hetty Pegler's Tump, Uley

Less than a mile north is Hetty Pegler's Tump, or Uley Long Barrow, a prehistoric burial mound containing a stone-built central passage with five chambers – two on either side and one at the end. It is named after the wife of a seventeenth-century owner of the land. Old guidebooks talk of the tomb being locked – the key to which could be obtained from a nearby cottage, together with the candle and matches essential for illuminating the dank, dark and sepulchral interior.

Cam Valley,

Cam and Dursley,

from Frocester Hill

Standing high on wooded Nibley Knoll – immediately above the village of North Nibley and overlooking the Vale of Berkeley and the River Severn – the Tyndale Monument was erected in 1866 to commemorate William Tyndale. He was the first translator of the Bible into English, and was burned at the stake as a heretic at Vilvorde, near Brussels, in 1536. Although a William Tyndale lived at North Nibley in the sixteenth century, it now seems this was not the same man, whose birthplace was somewhere further west 'on the borders of Wales'. The monument, sited some 650 feet above sea-level, is more than 110 feet tall. Rudder described the landscape east of Nibley Knoll in *A New History of Gloucestershire* (1779): 'Some part of it shoots up eastward over the hills between Wotton-under-Edge and Dursley, to the distance of near three miles from the church; and between those hills there is a long and narrow dingle, gradually opening towards the west, called Waterley Bottom, from a rivulet running down it. The

North Nibley and
Tyndale Monument,
from Stinchcombe Hill

steep sides of the hills in this part of the country are covered with beautiful hanging woods, in which the beech predominates; and the little coombs between them, of which there are many, are richly cultivated in small enclosures of pasture grounds, interspersed with here and there a cottage or a little dairy farm.' Nibley Green, situated below Nibley Knoll, is noted for being the site of the last private battle to be fought on English soil. Waged in 1470, between the rival claimants to the Berkeley estates, the conflict ended with the death of Thomas Talbot, Lord Lisle and victory for William, 6th Lord Berkeley. It was not until several centuries later, however, that the ownership dispute was finally settled, this time by more peaceable means.

Vale of Berkeley, from Nibley Knoll

Tyndale Monument, Nibley Knoll

Around North Nibley and Wotton-under-Edge the Cotswold escarpment has been eroded by landslips and water to create a series of deep coombs, known as 'bottoms'. Although little more than two miles east of Wotton, Ozleworth Bottom is secluded and remote, with only a single, narrow muddy lane – dark and overhung by trees – threading its way up the valley to the church and manor (but no village or hamlet). The little church of St Nicholas of Myra, standing alongside the eighteenth-century manor house of Ozleworth Park, has an irregular hexagonal Norman tower, which is a great rarity in the Cotswolds. Possibly occupying the site of an Anglo-Saxon foundation, the earliest part of the present church is thought to have been built by Roger de Berkeley (d.1131), who granted the patronage to the Augustinian priory at Leonard Stanley (which became a cell of Gloucester Abbey in 1146 and, thereafter, Ozleworth church remained a possession of the abbey until the Dissolution). The churchyard, which is surrounded by a high drystone wall, is unusual in being circular, and is some 150 feet in diameter. It has been suggested that this may indicate a pre-Christian sacred site.

Church and manor,
Ozleworth

Tetbury

Situated at a major crossroads, about two miles west of the Fosse Way, is the old market town of Tetbury. The town was once an important centre of the Cotswold wool trade, reaching the height of its prosperity in the sixteenth and seventeenth centuries. As such, it contains many buildings of great architectural interest – with numerous properties (despite their eighteenth- and nineteenth-century façades) dating back to Elizabethan times and even earlier. The Market House, or town hall, to which all streets of Tetbury lead, was erected in 1655 and enlarged the following century. It is supported on stone pillars. Tetbury's medieval fairs and animal markets were held at The Chipping, the lesser square situated north of the Market House. Soaring above the rooftops of the town, the tower and spire of the parish church of St Mary the Virgin reach a height of 186 feet. Although preserved when the church was rebuilt in the late eighteenth century, the tower and spire were dismantled and re-erected in Victorian times. Further restoration of the church was carried out between 1992 and 1993.

Three miles south-west of Tetbury is the village of Westonbirt, celebrated for its magnificent arboretum founded in 1829 by the estate owner, Robert Stayner Holford. Like many of the wealthy landed gentry, Holford commissioned plant hunters throughout the world to seek out and send back examples of rare and exotic trees for his collection. Although his greatest rival was the Earl of Ducie (at Tortworth, in the Vale of Berkeley to the west), their respective gardeners were reputed to have swapped plants as well as drinks in their local hostelries. Over the decades, Holford and his son, George, transformed the open pastures of the predominantly limestone plateau at Westonbirt into a tree-filled landscape of dramatic contrasts, with rides, glades and grassy 'Downs'. The Acer Glade in the Old Arboretum, for example, was created in the third quarter of the nineteenth century, and was often the setting for picnics and open-air entertainments. Today, the arboretum, covering an area of some 600 acres, is owned and managed by the Forestry Commission for the benefit of the nation. Westonbirt House, completed in 1878 (and now a private girls' school) was built by Robert Holford to replace his father's Regency mansion of 1823 (which, in turn, replaced an earlier manor house of the Elizabethan period).

Acer Glade, Westonbirt Arboretum

Acer Glade, Westonbirt Arboretum

Perched on a hill above the Bristol Avon, the old market town of Malmesbury dates from the Anglo-Saxon period, some 1,400 years ago. Tradition says that the settlement was founded by Maeldulph, a Celtic monk, who built a hermitage and school on the rocky, later fortified, site. One of his reputed pupils, St Aldhelm, became the first abbot of the newly founded abbey at Malmesbury in *c.*675. The present church – which contained the shrine of the saint – was begun in the twelfth century. Even before its dissolution in 1539, the building had began to collapse. In *c.*1540, Leland recorded that the central spire, 'a mighty high pyramis', 'fell dangerously in hominum memoria' and was not rebuilt. All that now remains of the abbey church is the nave (serving as the parish church) and the richly carved south porch – the latter considered to be one of the finest examples of Norman decorative stonework to be found in England. In the early eleventh century, according to the medieval chronicler William of Malmesbury, Eilmer, a monk of the abbey, fastened wings to his hands and feet and flew 'like Daedalus' from the top of a tower for more than a furlong (220 yards). He survived the flight, but 'broke his legs, and was lame ever after'. On the south-eastern outskirts of the Wiltshire town – by the river and close to the massive eighteenth-century Avon Mills (a converted silk mill) – stands St John's Almshouse, founded in 1694. The filled-in arch facing the street was originally the medieval gateway of the Priory of St John of Jerusalem.

St John's Almshouse, Malmesbury

Malmesbury Abbey

The villages of Great and Little Badminton lie on opposite sides of Badminton Park, some eight miles south-west of Tetbury. Badminton House, which is the seat of the Dukes of Beaufort, dates from the seventeenth century, with notable alterations and additions during the following century. Interestingly, the dimensions of the hall determined the size of the badminton court, for it was here that the shuttlecock game was first played in the 1860s. The park, with its herds of red and fallow deer, is the annual venue for the world-famous Badminton Horse Trials. Many of the farms and villages in the vicinity are part of the Beaufort estate. Great Badminton, with its wide main street, contains estate houses constructed during the eighteenth and nineteenth centuries, together with a row of almshouses built c.1714. The church of St Michael and All Angels dates from the late eighteenth century, and replaced a medieval foundation sited to the west. The fourteenth-century church of St Michael at Little Badminton stands on the north side of the village green, facing a dovecote and several farms and cottages, some stonetiled, others thatched. It is thought that the construction of the little church was interrupted by the Black Death in 1348, hence one of the windows being plainer than the rest.

Dovecote and church,

Little Badminton

The old post office,

Great Badminton

Set in a secluded hollow beside the fourteenth-century church of St James, six miles south of Wotton-under-Edge, Horton Court contains the remains of what is thought to be the oldest rectory in England. Dating from around the mid-twelfth century, the single-storey Norman hall, forming the north wing of the present house, contains a doorway on the north side that is directly opposite the priest's door of the church (only some six paces away). The manor house, adjoining the hall, was built in 1521 for William Knight, chaplain to Henry VIII and later Bishop of Bath and Wells. He was also responsible for constructing the detached Italian-style loggia, or ambulatory, in the garden of the house. Although owned by the National Trust, only the hall and loggia are open to the public.

Horton Court

East front, Dyrham Park

Some eight miles north of Bath, the country mansion of Dyrham Park (owned by the National Trust) lies in a sheltered coomb, high on the Cotswold escarpment, with extensive views over Bristol and the Severn plain. The name Dyrham is derived from the Old English *deor-hamm*, meaning 'deer' and 'well-watered valley'; or possibly 'deer enclosure'. Set in landscaped parkland, the house was built between 1691 and 1710 for William Blathwayt, who was Secretary of State to William III. Essentially it consists of two buildings, joined back to back: that facing west designed by a French architect, Samuel Hauduroy; and that facing east (including the orangery) by the distinguished English architect William Talman. Although the grounds of the mansion once contained a large terraced water garden, with statues, fountains, ornamental pools and cascades, it has now virtually vanished (apart from a

statue of Neptune and two modified ponds). Indeed, towards the close of the eighteenth century, Rudder wrote: 'The curious water-works, which were made at great expense, are much neglected and going to decay.' The church of St Peter, beside the mansion, dates from the thirteenth century and sports an early fifteenth-century Perpendicular tower. In 577, according to the Anglo-Saxon Chronicle, Dyrham was the site of a major battle fought between the Britons and Anglo-Saxons, the latter vanquishing the former and slaughtering three of their kings. In consequence, the cities of Bath, Cirencester and Gloucester (and much of the countryside around, including the lower Severn valley) fell to the conquerors. On Hinton Hill, north-west of Dyrham Park, are the earthwork remains of an Iron Age hillfort and, nearby, a series of medieval strip lynchets formed by ploughing on a slope.

Formerly a major centre of woollen cloth manufacture, boasting more than thirty cloth factories and countless looms in weavers' cottages, Bradford-on-Avon stands on the steep north bank of the Bristol Avon, some eleven miles downstream from Bath. Wealth from the cloth trade led to the building of many fine houses in the town, especially during the eighteenth century, when Daniel Defoe noted that the clothiers were reputedly 'worth from ten thousand to forty thousand pounds a man'. The Town Bridge dates from medieval times, but was largely rebuilt and widened in the seventeenth century. Its tiny domed chapel (later used as a lock-up and possibly a toll-house) sports a fish weather-vane – giving rise to the saying that the prisoners locked inside were 'under the fish and over

the water'. At Barton Farm, on the southern outskirts of the town, is an impressive monastic tithe barn, built in the early fourteenth century. Some 168 feet long and more than thirty feet wide, the slate-roofed building has four porches and a magnificent timber roof of fourteen bays. The barn is now in the care of English Heritage. Opposite the parish church of Holy Trinity (dating from Norman times, but essentially fourteenth century) stands the church of St Laurence. It was forgotten for centuries and re-discovered in 1856 – long after it had been converted into a cottage and school with buildings attached. Clearance of all the extraneous additions revealed one of the best-preserved Anglo-Saxon churches in the country. Other buildings of interest in the town are: The Hall, a clothier's mansion of c.1610; the chapel of St Mary, Tory, rebuilt in Victorian times on the site of a medieval hermitage; and Westbury House, scene of a riot against the introduction of new machinery in 1791.

Tithe barn,
Bradford-on-Avon

Dovecote, Barton Farm,
Bradford-on-Avon

Above Battlefields, situated on the windswept plateau of Lansdown Hill, north of Bath, stands a twenty-five-feet-high monument to Sir Bevil Grenville, killed in the Civil War battle of 1643. Attempting to attack the city, the Royalist army led by Sir Ralph Hopton reached Freezing Hill (just across the valley north of the monument) to find themselves opposed by Parliamentarian forces under Sir William Waller. After repulsing several attacks by Waller's men, a party of Royalists, led by Grenville, managed to cross the valley and gain the summit of Lansdown

Hamswell Valley &
Lansdown Hill

Freezing Hill, from
Nimlet Hill

Hill, which they held against all opposition. Joined by the rest of the Royalist army, Grenville's men eventually forced the Parliamentarians to retreat to Bath. In his moment of victory, however, Grenville was mortally wounded and died at nearby Cold Ashton. His monument, bearing the crest of the Grenville (later Granville) family, was erected in 1720 by his grandson, George Grenville, Lord Lansdown. East of the ridge is the Hamswell Valley, the head of which is crossed by the Cotswold Way before it climbs up to the summit of Lansdown Hill and heads south for Bath.

'If other cities are interesting as being old, Bath is not less so being new.

It has no aqueduct, no palaces, no gates, castle, or city walls,

yet it is the finest and most striking town that I have ever seen.'

ROBERT SOUTHEY, *LETTERS FROM ENGLAND* (1803)

Situated at the southernmost tip of the Cotswold escarpment, the 'golden city of Bath' rises tier upon tier from the winding valley of the Bristol Avon, with a glorious wealth of Georgian architecture created out of locally quarried honey-cream limestone. The city – which was designated a World Heritage site in 1987 – owes its origins to the warm, natural mineral springs that gush out of the ground beside the river. After discovering the therapeutic properties of the waters in the first century AD, the Romans built a town, Aquae Sulis, around the site, with elaborate baths and a temple dedicated to Sulis-Minerva – the healing goddess of the sacred springs (derived from Sulis, the Celtic water deity, and Minerva, the Roman

The Royal Crescent, Bath

goddess of war and wisdom). After the Romans left Britain in the early fifth century, the city fell into ruin along with the baths. Yet the springs continued to flow. It was not until the end of the nineteenth century that the Great Bath was rediscovered, still partly lined with Roman lead. The springs that feed the bath today flow at the rate of about 250,000 gallons a day at a constant temperature of 49°C (120°F). The transformation of the city into a fashionable and elegant Georgian spa town was essentially

Bath, from Alexandra Park

153

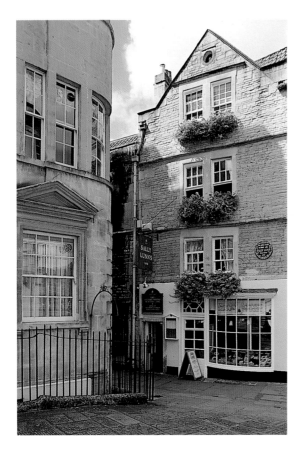

pastrycook, established what was to become the most fashionable place of refreshment in the city. Bath Abbey, standing on the site of several foundations dating back to Anglo-Saxon times, was erected at the close of the fifteenth century because of the dream of Oliver King, the Bishop of Bath and Wells. His vision of angels ascending and descending ladders to heaven is depicted in sculpted stone on the magnificent west front.

brought about by three self-made men: Richard 'Beau' Nash, who became Master of Ceremonies, publishing and enforcing a code of conduct for visitors; Ralph Allen, who became chief postmaster and owner of the quarries from which much of the city's building stone came; and John Wood the Elder, who was responsible for the design of many of the city's finest buildings, including the Crescent, begun in 1767. The Royal Victoria Park, in front of the Crescent, was laid out in 1830, Pultney Bridge (with shops on both sides) was erected in 1770 and the Pump Room was rebuilt in the 1790s. The oldest house in the city is reputed to be Sally Lunn's House, dating from *c.*1480. It was here in the 1680s that Sally Lunn, the French

Sally Lunn's house, Bath

The Great Bath, Roman baths, Bath

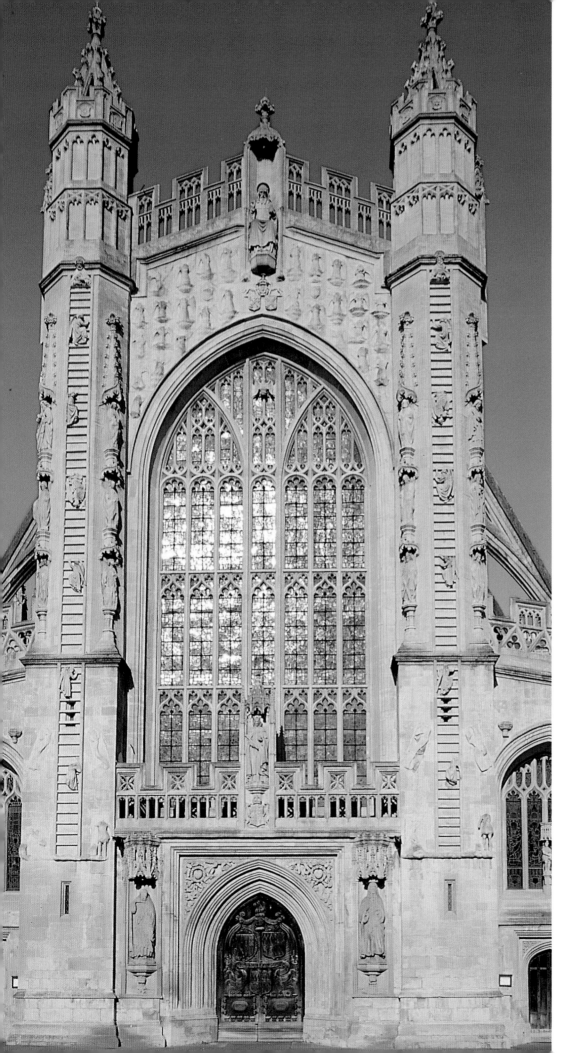

On a still summer's evening, when the sky is clear of cloud, the slanting rays of the sun strike the oolitic limestone of Bath Abbey's west front to illuminate the heavenly stairway with a light that is truly magical: a light that seems to shine from within the granular structure of the stone itself; a light that shifts and changes with each variation in the weather; a light – warm, golden and harmonious – that is unique to the buildings and landscape of the Cotswolds, whether in Bath, Oxford, or the farms, villages and towns that lie between.

West front, Bath Abbey

PHOTOGRAPHIC INFORMATION

The photographic information refers to:
Make and type of camera; Film size; Film
stock (all Fuji); Tripod or Handheld; Lens;
f stop; shutter speed; Polarizing filter (if used).
All lenses had a filter attached, primarily to
protect the front element, but chosen to have
a slight warming quality.
The tripod was an amazingly light, but very
strong, carbon-fibre Gitzo, and the light meter
a handheld Seconic. All equipment was
carried in standard rucksacks.
Film processing was by Colab, Coventry.

1 Nikon F3; 35mm; Velvia; Handheld;
28mm; f5.6; 1/125 sec

2 Hasselblad 503CX; 6x6; Provia; Tripod;
50mm; f22; 1/4 sec; Polarizer

6-7 Nikon F3; 35mm; Velvia; Handheld;
28mmPC; f5.6; 1/125 sec

8 Hasselblad 503CX; 6x6; Provia; Tripod;
150mm; f22; 1/15 sec

11 Nikon F3; 35mm; Velvia; Handheld;
24mm; f5.6; 1/125 sec

12 Nikon F3; 35mm; Velvia; Handheld;
24mm; f4; 1/60 sec; Polarizer

13 Nikon F3; 35mm; Velvia; Handheld;
35mm; f8; 1/60 sec

14 Nikon F3; 35mm; Velvia; Handheld;
28mmPC; f8; 1/60 sec

16 Hasselblad 503CX; 6x6; Provia; Tripod;
50mm; f22; 1/4 sec; Polarizer

17 Nikon F3; 35mm; Velvia; Handheld;
24mm; f5.6; 1/60 sec

18 Nikon F3; 35mm; Velvia; Handheld;
28mmPC; f8; 1/60 sec

19 Nikon F3; 35mm; Velvia; Handheld;
28mmPC; f8; 1/60 sec

22-23 Nikon F3; 35mm; Velvia; Handheld;
24mm; f4; 1/60 sec; Polarizer

24 (top) Nikon F3; 35mm; Velvia; Handheld;
24mm; f4; 1/60 sec; Polarizer

24 (bottom) Nikon F3; 35mm; Velvia;
Handheld; 28mmPC; f8; 1/60 sec

25 (top) Nikon F3; 35mm; Velvia; Handheld;
85mm; f5.6; 1/125 sec

25 (bottom) Nikon F3; 35mm; Velvia;
Handheld; 28mmPC; f8; 1/60 sec

26 (top) Nikon F3; 35mm; Velvia; Handheld;
24mm; f8; 1/60 sec

26 (bottom) Nikon F3; 35mm; Velvia;
Handheld; 28mmPC; f8; 1/60 sec

27 Nikon F3; 35mm; Velvia; Handheld;
85mm; f8; 1/60 sec

28 Nikon F3; 35mm; Velvia; Handheld;
28mmPC; f8; 1/60 sec

28-29 Nikon F3; 35mm; Velvia; Handheld;
180mm; f5.6; 1/125 sec

30-31 Nikon F3; 35mm; Velvia; Handheld;
35mm; f5.6; 1/60 sec

31 (top) Nikon F3; 35mm; Velvia; Handheld;
85mm; f5.6; 1/60 sec

31 (bottom) Nikon F3; 35mm; Velvia;
Handheld; 85mm; f5.6; 1/60 sec

32 Nikon F3; 35mm; Velvia; Tripod;
180mm; f22; 1/15 sec

32-33 Hasselblad 503CX; 6x6; Provia;
Tripod; 50mm; f22; 1/4 sec; Polarizer

34 Nikon F3; 35mm; Velvia; Handheld;
28mmPC; f8; 1/60 sec

35 Hasselblad 503CX; 6x6; Provia; Tripod;
50mm; f22; 1/4 sec; Polarizer

36 Nikon F3; 35mm; Velvia; Handheld;
85mm; f8; 1/60 sec

37 (top) Nikon F3; 35mm; Velvia; Handheld;
35mm; f5.6; 1/60 sec; Polarizer

37 (bottom) Nikon F3; 35mm; Velvia;
Handheld; 85mm; f8; 1/60 sec

38 Nikon F3; 35mm; Velvia; Handheld;
180mm; f5.6; 1/60 sec

39 Nikon F3; 35mm; Velvia; Handheld;
180mm; f5.6; 1/125 sec

40 Nikon F3; 35mm; Velvia; Handheld;
180mm; f5.6; 1/125 sec

41 Hasselblad 503CX; 6x6; Provia; Tripod;
50mm; f22; 1/4 sec; Polarizer

42 Nikon F3; 35mm; Velvia; Handheld;
28mmPC; f8; 1/60 sec

43 Nikon F3; 35mm; Velvia; Handheld;
28mmPC; f8; 1/60 sec

44 Nikon F3; 35mm; Velvia; Handheld;
28mmPC; f8; 1/60 sec

45 Nikon F3; 35mm; Velvia; Tripod;
180mm; f22; 1/8 sec

46 Nikon F3; 35mm; Velvia; Handheld;
28mmPC; f8; 1/60 sec

47 (top) Nikon F3; 35mm; Velvia; Handheld;
85mm; f8; 1/60 sec

47 (bottom) Nikon F3; 35mm; Velvia;
Handheld; 24mm; f8; 1/60 sec

48 Nikon F3; 35mm; Velvia; Handheld;
28mmPC; f8; 1/60 sec

48-49 Nikon F3; 35mm; Velvia; Handheld;
28mmPC; f8; 1/60 sec

50 Nikon F3; 35mm; Velvia; Handheld;
28mmPC; f8; 1/60 sec

51 Hasselblad 503CX; 6x6; Provia; Tripod;
150mm; f22; 1/4 sec; Polarizer

52 Hasselblad 503CX; 6x6; Provia; Tripod;
150mm; f22; 1/4 sec; Polarizer

53 (top) Nikon F3; 35mm; Velvia; Handheld;
28mmPC; f8; 1/60 sec

53 (bottom) Hasselblad 503CX; 6x6; Provia;
Tripod; 150mm; f22; 1/4 sec; Polarizer

54 (top) Hasselblad 503CX; 6x6; Provia;
Tripod; 50mm; f22; 1/4 sec; Polarizer

54 (bottom) Hasselblad 503CX; 6x6; Provia;
Tripod; 150mm; f22; 1/4 sec; Polarizer

55 Hasselblad 503CX; 6x6; Provia; Tripod;
50mm; f22; 1/4 sec; Polarizer

56 Nikon F3; 35mm; Velvia; Handheld;
28mmPC; f8; 1/60 sec

57 (top) Nikon F3; 35mm; Velvia; Handheld;
28mm; f5.6; 1/125 sec

57 (bottom) Nikon F3; 35mm; Velvia;
Handheld; 24mm; f5.6; 1/60 sec; Polarizer

58 Hasselblad 503CX; 6x6; Provia; Tripod;
80mm; f22; 1/4 sec; Polarizer

59 Hasselblad 503CX; 6x6; Provia; Tripod;
150mm; f22; 1/15 sec

60 Nikon F3; 35mm; Velvia; Handheld;
28mmPC; f8; 1/60 sec

61 Hasselblad 503CX; 6x6; Provia; Tripod;
80mm; f22; 1/4 sec; Polarizer

62 Nikon F3; 35mm; Velvia; Tripod;
180mm; f22; 1/8 sec

63 (top) Nikon F3; 35mm; Velvia; Handheld;
24mm; f5.6; 1/60 sec

63 (bottom) Nikon F3; 35mm; Velvia;
Handheld; 28mmPC; f8; 1/60 sec

64 Nikon F3; 35mm; Velvia; Handheld;
85mm; f8; 1/60 sec

65 (top) Nikon F3; 35mm; Velvia; Handheld;
28mmPC; f8; 1/60 sec

65 (bottom) Nikon F3; 35mm; Velvia;
Handheld; 85mm; f8; 1/60 sec

66-67 Hasselblad 503CX; 6x6; Provia;
Tripod; 50mm; f22; 1/4 sec; Polarizer

67 Hasselblad 503CX; 6x6; Provia; Tripod;
50mm; f22; 1/4 sec; Polarizer

68 Nikon F3; 35mm; Velvia; Handheld;
180mm; f5.6; 1/125 sec

69 (top) Nikon F3; 35mm; Velvia; Handheld;
85mm; f8; 1/60 sec

69 (bottom) Nikon F3; 35mm; Velvia;
Handheld; 28mmPC; f8; 1/60 sec

70-71 Nikon F3; 35mm; Velvia; Handheld;
85mm; f8; 1/60 sec

72 (top) Nikon F3; 35mm; Velvia; Handheld;
85mm; f8; 1/60 sec

72 (bottom) Nikon F3; 35mm; Velvia;
Handheld; 28mmPC; f8; 1/60 sec

73 Nikon F3; 35mm; Velvia; Handheld;
180mm; f5.6; 1/125 sec

74 Nikon F3; 35mm; Velvia; Handheld;
28mmPC; f8; 1/60 sec

75 Nikon F3; 35mm; Velvia; Handheld;
28mmPC; f8; 1/60 sec

76 Nikon F3; 35mm; Velvia; Handheld;
28mmPC; f8; 1/60 sec

77 Nikon F3; 35mm; Velvia; Handheld;
85mm; f8; 1/60 sec

78 Nikon F3; 35mm; Velvia; Handheld;
28mmPC; f8; 1/60 sec

79 Nikon F3; 35mm; Velvia; Handheld;
85mm; f8; 1/60 sec

80 Nikon F3; 35mm; Velvia; Handheld;
35mm; f8; 1/60 sec

81 (top) Nikon F3; 35mm; Velvia; Handheld;
28mmPC; f8; 1/60 sec

81 (bottom) Nikon F3; 35mm; Velvia;
Handheld; 28mmPC; f8; 1/60 sec

82-83 Nikon F3; 35mm; Velvia; Handheld;
24mm; f4; 1/60 sec; Polarizer

83 Nikon F3; 35mm; Velvia; Handheld;
24mm; f4; 1/60 sec; Polarizer

84-85 Hasselblad 503CX; 6x6; Provia;
Tripod; 50mm; f22; 1/4 sec; Polarizer

86-87 Nikon F3; 35mm; Velvia; Handheld;
85mm; f4; 1/60 sec; Polarizer

87 Nikon F3; 35mm; Velvia; Handheld;
24mm; f8; 1/60 sec

88 Nikon F3; 35mm; Velvia; Handheld;
85mm; f5.6; 1/125 sec

89 Hasselblad 503CX; 6x6; Provia; Tripod;
50mm; f22; 1/15 sec

90 Nikon F3; 35mm; Velvia; Handheld;
28mmPC; f5.6; 1/125 sec

91 Hasselblad 503CX; 6x6; Provia; Tripod;
150mm; f22; 1/15 sec

92 Hasselblad 503CX; 6x6; Provia; Tripod;
50mm; f22; 1/15 sec

93 Hasselblad 503CX; 6x6; Provia; Tripod;
150mm; f22; 1/4 sec

94 Nikon F3; 35mm; Velvia; Handheld;
28mmPC; f5.6; 1/125 sec

95 Nikon F3; 35mm; Velvia; Handheld;
28mmPC; f8; 1/60 sec

96 Nikon F3; 35mm; Velvia; Handheld;
28mmPC; f8; 1/60 sec

97 (top) Nikon F3; 35mm; Velvia; Handheld;
28mmPC; f8; 1/60 sec

97 (bottom) Nikon F3; 35mm; Velvia; Tripod;
85mm; f22; 1/8 sec

98-99 Nikon F3; 35mm; Velvia; Handheld;
28mmPC; f8; 1/60 sec

99 Nikon F3; 35mm; Velvia; Handheld;
28mmPC; f8; 1/60 sec

100 Nikon F3; 35mm; Velvia; Handheld;
28mmPC; f8; 1/60 sec

100-101 Hasselblad 503CX; 6x6; Provia;
Tripod; 150mm; f22; 1/15 sec

102-103 Nikon F3; 35mm; Velvia; Handheld;
180mm; f5.6; 1/125 sec

104 Hasselblad 503CX; 6x6; Provia; Tripod;
50mm; f22; 1/4 sec; Polarizer

105 Nikon F3; 35mm; Velvia; Handheld;
85mm; f5.6; 1/125 sec

106-107 Hasselblad 503CX; 6x6; Provia;
Tripod; 50mm; f22; 1/4 sec; Polarizer

108-109 Hasselblad 503CX; 6x6; Provia;
Tripod; 50mm; f22; 1/15 sec

110 (left) Nikon F3; 35mm; Velvia; Handheld;
28mmPC; f8; 1/60 sec

110 (right) Hasselblad 503CX; 6x6; Provia;
Tripod; 50mm; f22; 1/15 sec

111 Hasselblad 503CX; 6x6; Provia; Tripod;
150mm; f22; 1/4 sec; Polarizer

112 Hasselblad 503CX; 6x6; Provia; Tripod;
50mm; f22;   1/4 sec; Polarizer

113 (left) Nikon F3; 35mm; Velvia; Handheld;
28mmPC; f8; 1/60 sec

113 (right) Nikon F3; 35mm; Velvia;
Handheld; 28mmPC; f8; 1/60 sec

114 (top) Nikon F3; 35mm; Velvia; Handheld;
28mmPC; f5.6; 1/30 sec; Polarizer

114 (bottom) Nikon F3; 35mm; Velvia;
Handheld; 28mmPC; f5.6; 1/30 sec; Polarizer

115 Nikon F3; 35mm; Velvia; Handheld;
28mmPC; f8; 1/60 sec

116 Nikon F3; 35mm; Velvia; Handheld;
28mmPC; f8; 1/60 sec

117 Hasselblad 503CX; 6x6; Provia; Tripod;
150mm; f22; 1/15 sec

118 (top) Nikon F3; 35mm; Velvia; Handheld;
28mmPC; f8; 1/60 sec

118 (bottom) Nikon F3; 35mm; Velvia;
Handheld; 24mm; f8; 1/60 sec

119 Nikon F3; 35mm; Velvia; Handheld;
28mmPC; f8; 1/60 sec

120 Nikon F3; 35mm; Velvia; Handheld;
28mmPC; f8; 1/60 sec

121 Nikon F3; 35mm; Velvia; Handheld;
28mmPC; f8; 1/60 sec

122 Nikon F3; 35mm; Velvia; Handheld;
28mmPC; f8; 1/60 sec

123 Hasselblad 503CX; 6x6; Provia; Tripod;
50mm; f16; 1/30 sec

124 Nikon F3; 35mm; Velvia; Handheld;
28mmPC; f8; 1/60 sec

125 (top) Nikon F3; 35mm; Velvia; Handheld;
28mmPC; f8; 1/60 sec

125 (bottom) Nikon F3; 35mm; Velvia;
Handheld; 28mmPC; f8; 1/60 sec

126 Nikon F3; 35mm; Velvia; Handheld;
28mmPC; f8; 1/60 sec

127 Hasselblad 503CX; 6x6; Provia; Tripod;
150mm; f22; 1/4 sec; Polarizer

128-129 Hasselblad 503CX; 6x6; Provia;
Tripod; 50mm; f22; 1/4 sec; Polarizer

130-131 Hasselblad 503CX; 6x6; Provia;
Tripod; 50mm; f22; 1/4 sec; Polarizer

131 Nikon F3; 35mm; Velvia; Handheld;
24mm; f8; 1/60 sec

132-133 Hasselblad 503CX; 6x6; Provia;
Tripod; 150mm; f22; 1/15 sec

134 Hasselblad 503CX; 6x6; Provia; Tripod;
50mm; f22; 1/15 sec

135 (top) Hasselblad 503CX; 6x6; Provia;
Tripod; 50mm; f22; 1/4 sec; Polarizer

135 (bottom) Nikon F3; 35mm; Velvia;
Handheld; 24mm; f8; 1/60 sec

136-137 Hasselblad 503CX; 6x6; Provia;
Tripod; 80mm; f22; 1/4 sec

137 (top) Hasselblad 503CX; 6x6; Provia;
Tripod; 50mm; f22; 1/15 sec

137 (bottom) Hasselblad 503CX; 6x6; Provia;
Tripod; 50mm; f22; 1/15 sec

138 Nikon F3; 35mm; Velvia; Handheld;
28mmPC; f8; 1/60 sec

139 Nikon F3; 35mm; Velvia; Handheld;
24mm; f5.6; 1/60 sec; Polarizer

140 Hasselblad 503CX; 6x6; Provia; Tripod;
150mm; f22; 1/8 sec

141 Hasselblad 503CX; 6x6; Provia; Tripod;
150mm; f22; 1/8 sec

142 Nikon F3; 35mm; Velvia; Handheld;
28mmPC; f8; 1/60 sec

143 Nikon F3; 35mm; Velvia; Handheld;
28mmPC; f8; 1/60 sec

144 (top) Nikon F3; 35mm; Velvia; Handheld;
60mm; f8; 1/60 sec

144 (bottom) Nikon F3; 35mm; Velvia;
Handheld; 60mm; f8; 1/60 sec

145 Nikon F3; 35mm; Velvia; Handheld;
28mmPC; f8; 1/60 sec

146 Nikon F3; 35mm; Velvia; Handheld;
85mm; f5.6; 1/125 sec

147 Nikon F3; 35mm; Velvia; Handheld;
28mmPC; f8; 1/60 sec

148 Nikon F3; 35mm; Velvia; Handheld;
28mmPC; f8; 1/60 sec

149 (top) Nikon F3; 35mm; Velvia; Handheld;
24mm; f8; 1/60 sec

149 (bottom) Nikon F3; 35mm; Velvia;
Handheld; 180mm; f4; 1/250 sec

150-151 Nikon F3; 35mm; Velvia; Handheld;
85mm; f5.6; 1/60 sec

151 Hasselblad 503CX; 6x6; Provia; Tripod;
150mm; f22; 1/4 sec; Polarizer

152 Nikon F3; 35mm; Velvia; Handheld;
180mm; f5.6; 1/125 sec

153 Nikon F3; 35mm; Velvia; Handheld;
28mmPC; f8; 1/60 sec

154 (left) Nikon F3; 35mm; Velvia; Handheld;
28mmPC; f8; 1/60 sec

154 (right) Nikon F3; 35mm; Velvia;
Handheld; 24mm; f8; 1/60 sec

155 Nikon F3; 35mm; Velvia; Handheld;
28mmPC; f8; 1/60 sec

English Heritage

HISTORIC PROPERTIES SOUTH-EAST
1 High Street
Tonbridge
Kent TN9 1SG
Telephone: (01732) 778028

HISTORIC PROPERTIES SOUTH-WEST
29 Queens Square
Bristol BS1 4ND
Telephone: (0117) 9750700

HAILES ABBEY
nr. Winchcombe
Cheltenham
Gloucestershire GL54 5PB
Telephone: 01242 602398
Open: April to end October daily;
November to end March, Saturdays & Sundays;
closed 24–26 December & New Years Day.

MINSTER LOVELL HALL
Minster Lovell
Oxfordshire
Open: daily throughout the year,
at any reasonable time.

National Trust

SEVERN REGIONAL OFFICE
Mythe End House
Tewkesbury
Gloucestershire GL20 6EB
Telephone: (01684) 850051

THAMES & CHILTERNS REGIONAL OFFICE
Hughenden Manor
High Wycombe
Buckinghamshire HP14 4LA
Telephone: (01494) 528051

WESSEX REGIONAL OFFICE
Eastleigh Court
Bishopstrow
Warminster
Wiltshire BA12 9HW
Telephone: (01985) 843600

CHASTLETON HOUSE
Chastleton
Moreton-in-Marsh
Oxfordshire GL56 0SU
Telephone: (01608) 674284
Open: April to end October, Wednesdays
to Saturdays (pre-booked timed ticket only).

CHEDWORTH ROMAN VILLA
Yanworth
nr. Cheltenham
Gloucestershire GL54 3LJ
Telephone: (01242) 890256
Open: March to end November daily, except
Mondays (but open Bank Holiday Mondays).

DYRHAM PARK
nr. Chippenham
South Gloucestershire SN14 8ER
Telephone: (0117) 9372501
House & Garden open April to end October daily,
Fridays to Tuesdays; park open daily all year,
except Christmas Day.

HIDCOTE MANOR GARDEN
Hidcote Bartrim
nr. Chipping Campden
Gloucestershire GL55 6LR
Telephone: (01386) 438333
Open: April to end October, daily
except Tuesdays and Fridays;
also open Tuesdays in June and July.

HORTON COURT
nr. Chipping Sodbury
Bristol BS17 6QR
Telephone: Regional Office (01985) 843600
Open: April to end October, Wednesdays
and Saturdays.

SNOWSHILL MANOR
Snowshill
nr. Broadway
Worcestershire WR12 7LU
Telephone: (01386) 852410
Open: April to end October, Wednesdays
to Mondays; closed Good Fridays.

Miscellaneous

BLENHEIM PALACE
Woodstock
Oxfordshire OX20 1PX
Telephone: (01993) 811091
Open: Palace, mid-March to end October daily;
Park, open daily throughout the year.

BROADWAY TOWER COUNTRY PARK
Broadway
Worcestershire W12 7LB
Telephone: 01386 852390
Open: April to end October daily;
also during winter months, especially at weekends
(but please check beforehand since opening times
depend on the weather).

COTSWOLD FARM PARK
nr. Guiting Power
Cheltenham
Gloucestershire GL54 5UG
Telephone: (01451) 850307
Open: April to end September daily.

KELMSCOTT MANOR
Kelmscott
nr. Lechlade
Oxfordshire GL7 3HU
Telephone: 01367 252486
Open: April to end September, Wednesdays and
third Saturday in each month; pre-booked group
visits can be arranged on Thursdays and Fridays.

OWLPEN MANOR
Owlpen
nr. Uley
Gloucestershire GL11 5BZ
Telephone: (01453) 860261
Open: April to end October, Tuesdays to Sundays
& Bank Holiday Mondays.

ROMAN BATHS MUSEUM
Pump Room
Abbey Churchyard
Bath BA1 1LZ
Telephone: (01225) 477785
Open: daily throughout the year,
except 25 & 26 December.

SHELDONIAN THEATRE
Broad Street
Oxford OX1 3AZ
Telephone: (01865) 277299

STANWAY HOUSE
Stanway
Cheltenham
Gloucestershire GL54 5PQ
Telephone: (01386) 584469
Open: June to September, Tuesdays & Thursdays.

SUDELEY CASTLE
Winchcombe
Cheltenham
Gloucestershire GL54 5JD
Telephone: (01242) 602308
Open: end March to end October daily.

WESTONBIRT ARBORETUM
Westonbirt
Tetbury
Gloucestershire GL8 8QS
Telephone: (01666) 880220
Open: Arboretum, daily throughout the year; Visitor
Centre, daily, except for one week at Christmas.

Briggs, Katherine M, *The Folklore of the Cotswolds*, Batsford, London, 1974

Brill, Edith, *Cotswold Crafts*, Batsford, London, 1977

Brill, Edith, *Life & Tradition on the Cotswolds*, Dent, London, 1973

Brill, Edith, *Portrait of the Cotswolds*, Hale, London, 1964

Brill, Edith, & Turner, Peter, *The Minor Pleasures of Cotswold*, Dent, London, 1971

Burton, Anthony, *The Cotswold Way*, Aurum Press, London, 1995

Camden, William, *Britannia*, Gibson, Oxford, 1695 (1st pub. 1586)

Carroll, David, *A Literary Tour of Gloucestershire & Bristol*, Sutton, Stroud, 1994

Clark, Sir George, (ed.), *The Campden Wonder*, OUP, London, 1959

Cobbett, William, *Rural Rides*, Dent, London, 1912

Colyer, S W, *Cotswold Country*, Ward Lock, London, 1939

Cumming, Elizabeth, & Kaplan, Wendy, *The Arts & Crafts Movement*, Thames & Hudson, London, 1991

Defoe, Daniel, *A Tour Thro' the Whole Island of Great Britain*, Peter Davies, London, 1927

Derrick, Freda, *Cotswold Stone*, Chapman & Hall, London, 1948

Dreghorn, William, *Geology Explained in the Severn Vale & Cotswolds*, David & Charles, Newton Abbot, 1967

Eales, Ernest Frederic, *Naunton Upon Cotswold*, Alden Press, Oxford, 1928

Evans, Herbert A, *Highways & Byways in Oxford & the Cotswolds*, Macmillan, London, 1923

Exell, A W, *Joanna Southcott at Blockley and The Rock Cottage Relics*, Blockley Antiquarian Society, Blockley, 1977

Finsberg, Josceline, *The Cotswolds (Regions of Britain)*, Eyre Methuen, London, 1977

Fortey, Richard, *The Hidden Landscape*, Cape, London, 1993

Garrett, John Henry, *From a Cotswold Height*, Banks, Cheltenham, 1919

Gibbs, J Arthur, *A Cotswold Village*, Murray, London, 1898

Gordon, Caroline, *Gazetteer of Arts & Crafts Architecture in the Cotswold Region*, Cheltenham Art Gallery & Museums, Cheltenham, 1992

Greensted, Mary, *The Arts & Crafts Movement in the Cotswolds*, Sutton, Stroud, 1993

Hadfield, Charles & Alice Mary, *Introducing the Cotswolds*, David & Charles, Newton Abbot, 1976

Hadfield, Charles & Alice Mary, *The Cotswolds: A New Study*, David & Charles, Newton Abbot, 1973

Hawthorne, Nathaniel, *Our Old Home: A Series of English Sketches*, Paterson, Edinburgh, nd

Hill, Michael, & Birch, Sally, *Cotswold Stone Homes*, Sutton, Stroud, 1994

Jarvis, Janet, *Christopher Wren's Cotswold Masons*, Thornhill Press, Cheltenham, 1980

Johnson, Joan, *Towns & Villages of England: Stow-on-the-Wold*, Sutton, Stroud, 1994

Longhurst, Sybil, & others, *Sherborne: A Cotswold Village*, Sutton, Stroud, 1992

Macarthur, Wilson, *The River Windrush*, Cassell, London, 1946

MacCarthy, Fiona, *The Simple Life: C R Ashbee in the Cotswolds*, Lund Humphries, London, 1981

MacCarthy, Fiona, *William Morris: A Life For Our Time*, Faber & Faber, London, 1994

Massingham, H J, *Cotswold Country* (Face of Britain series), Batsford, London, 1937

Massingham, H J, *Wold Without End*, Cobden-Sanderson, London, 1932

Mee, Arthur, (ed.), *Gloucestershire* (King's England series), Hodder & Stoughton, London, 1938

Mee, Arthur, (ed.), *Oxfordshire* (King's England series), Hodder & Stoughton, London, 1942

Millward, Roy, & Robinson, Adrian, *The Avon Valley & the Cotswold Edge*, Macmillan, London, 1971

Mongomery-Massingberd, Hugh, *Blenheim Revisited*, Bodley Head, London, 1985

Monk, William J, *Northleach & Around*, Monk, nd

Moore, John, *The Cotswolds*, Chapman & Hall, London, 1937

Moriarty, Denis, *Buildings of the Cotswolds*, Gollancz, London, 1989

Murray, Alison D, *The Cotswolds*, British Publishing, Gloucester, 1930

Payne, Gordon E, *Gloucestershire: a Physical, Social & Economic Survey & Plan*, Gloucestershire County Council, nd

Pevsner, Nikolaus, *North Somerset & Bristol* (Buildings of England series), Penguin Books, Harmondsworth, 1958

Pevsner, Nikolaus, *Wiltshire* (Buildings of England series), Penguin Books, Harmondsworth, 1963 (rev. 1975)

Pevsner, Nikolaus, & Wedgwood, Alexandra, *Warwickshire* (Buildings of England series), Penguin Books, Harmondsworth, 1966

Powell, Geoffrey, *The Book of Campden*, Barracuda Books, Buckingham, 1982

Powell, W R, *Bradford-on-Avon: A History to 1950, Victoria History of Wiltshire*, University of London, London, 1953

Priestley, J B, *English Journey*, Heinemann, London, 1934

Randall, J, *The Severn Valley*, Virtue, London, 1862

Rudder, Samuel, *A New History of Gloucestershire*, Sutton, Gloucester, 1977 (1st pub. 1779)

Sherwood, Jennifer, & Pevsner, Nikolaus, *Oxfordshire* (Buildings of England series), Penguin Books, Harmondsworth, 1974

Sitwell, Edith, *Bath*, Faber & Faber, London, 1932

Tann, Jennifer, *Gloucestershire Woollen Mills*, David & Charles, Newton Abbot, 1967

Verey, David, *Gloucestershire: The Cotswolds* (Buildings of England series), Penguin Books, Harmondsworth, 1970

Verey, David, *Gloucestershire: The Vale & the Forest of Dean* (Buildings of England series), Penguin Books, Harmondsworth, 1970

Vyvyan, E R, *Cotswold Games: Annalia Dubrensia*, Tabard Press, London, 1970 (1st pub. 1878)

Warren, C Henry, *A Cotswolds Year*, Sutton, Gloucester, 1985

Waters, Brian, *Thirteen Rivers to the Thames*, Dent, London, 1964

Whiteman, Robin, & Talbot, Rob, *The Cotswolds*, Weidenfeld & Nicolson, London, 1987

Whitfield, Christopher, *A History of Chipping Campden*, Shakespeare Head Press, Windsor, 1958

Witts, Reverend F E, (Verey, David [ed.]), *The Diary of a Cotswold Parson*, Alan Sutton, Gloucester, 1978

Wray, Tony, & Stratford, David, *Bourton on the Water*, Alan Sutton, Stroud, 1994

Wright, Geoffrey N, *The Cotswolds*, David & Charles, Newton Abbot, 1991

Young, Arthur, *General View of the Agriculture of Oxfordshire*, Sherwood, Neely & Jones, London, 1813